RESTORATIVE JUSTICE CIRCLES

Healing Through Community Support

Dr. Maxwell Shimba

Printed in the United States of America

SHIMBA
PUBLISHING

TABLE OF CONTENTS

INTRODUCTION

Introduction to Restorative Justice Circles

By Dr. Maxwell Shimba

In a world where conflict and harm are often met with retribution and punishment, the need for an alternative approach to justice has never been more pressing. Restorative justice circles offer a transformative path, one that emphasizes healing, accountability, and the restoration of relationships. This book explores the profound impact of restorative justice circles, providing a comprehensive guide to understanding, implementing, and sustaining these practices in various settings.

The Essence of Restorative Justice Circles

Restorative justice circles are rooted in ancient traditions and practices found in diverse cultures around the world. At their core, these circles provide a space for individuals to come together, share their experiences, and collaboratively seek solutions to repair harm. Unlike the conventional justice system, which often focuses on punishment, restorative justice prioritizes the needs of victims, offenders, and the community, fostering a sense of collective responsibility and mutual support.

In restorative justice circles, every participant's voice is valued equally, creating an environment where empathy and understanding can flourish. The process encourages offenders to take responsibility for their actions, understand the impact of their behavior, and make amends. For victims, it offers a chance to be heard, express their feelings, and play an active role in the resolution process. Community members, too, are engaged, recognizing their role in supporting both the victim and the offender, and in promoting a harmonious and just society.

The Journey to Restorative Justice

My journey into the world of restorative justice circles began many years ago, driven by a deep conviction that our traditional systems of justice often fall short in addressing the root causes of harm and fostering true healing. Through my work with diverse communities and institutions, I have witnessed firsthand the transformative power of restorative justice circles. These experiences have reinforced my belief that this approach holds the potential to reshape our understanding of justice and create more compassionate and resilient communities.

This book is a culmination of years of research, practice, and reflection. It is designed to serve as both an introduction to those new to restorative justice circles and a comprehensive resource for experienced practitioners. Throughout these pages, you will find theoretical insights, practical guidance, and real-world examples that illustrate the profound impact of restorative justice circles.

Structure of the Book

The book is organized into several chapters, each focusing on a different aspect of restorative justice circles.

Chapter 1: Introduction to Restorative Justice provides an overview of restorative justice principles and the role of circles in fostering community healing. It explains what restorative justice circles are, where they can be found, and who arranges them.

Chapter 2: Principles of Restorative Justice Circles delves into the core principles guiding these circles, such as inclusivity, voluntariness, respect and equality, accountability, reparation, and reintegration.

Chapter 3: The History and Evolution of Restorative Justice traces the origins of restorative justice, highlighting its development from ancient practices to modern applications, and key milestones in the restorative justice movement.

Chapter 4: Implementing Restorative Justice Circles in Communities offers practical steps for introducing restorative justice circles into communities, including community assessment, building partnerships, training facilitators, and creating guidelines.

Chapter 5: The Role of Facilitators in Restorative Justice Circles discusses the qualities, skills, responsibilities, and training required for effective facilitation.

Chapter 6: The Circle Process: Steps and Procedures breaks down the restorative justice circle process into detailed steps, including preparation, opening, sharing, discussion, agreement, and closing.

Chapter 7: Case Studies: Success Stories from Restorative Justice Circles presents real-world examples demonstrating the effectiveness of restorative justice circles in various settings.

Chapter 8: Challenges and Solutions in Restorative Justice Circles identifies common obstacles and offers strategies for overcoming them, ensuring successful implementation and sustainability.

Chapter 9: The Psychological and Emotional Impact of Restorative Justice explores the benefits and potential risks of restorative justice circles on participants' psychological and emotional well-being.

Chapter 10: Restorative Justice Circles in Schools examines how circles can resolve disputes, improve student behavior, and create a supportive school culture.

Chapter 11: Restorative Justice Circles in the Workplace explores their application in professional settings to address grievances, improve communication, and foster a collaborative culture.

Chapter 12: Restorative Justice Circles in the Criminal Justice System discusses their use as an alternative to punitive measures, their potential to reduce recidivism, and support rehabilitation.

Chapter 13: Cultural and Global Perspectives on Restorative Justice Circles highlights global practices and adaptations, demonstrating their universal applicability.

Chapter 14: Building and Sustaining Restorative Communities offers guidance on sustaining restorative practices, fostering community involvement, and ensuring the longevity of restorative justice circles.

Chapter 15: Future Directions for Restorative Justice Circles explores emerging trends, potential advancements, and future directions for these practices.

A Call to Action

As you embark on this journey through the pages of this book, I invite you to open your mind and heart to the possibilities that restorative justice circles offer. Whether you are a community leader, educator, justice system professional, or someone seeking to make a positive difference, you will find valuable insights and practical tools to support your efforts.

Restorative justice circles challenge us to rethink our approach to justice, to prioritize healing over punishment, and to recognize our interconnectedness. By embracing these principles and practices, we can create more just, compassionate, and resilient communities.

Thank you for joining me on this journey. I hope that this book inspires you to explore, implement, and sustain restorative justice circles in your community, and to contribute to a world where healing and justice go hand in hand.

Dr. Maxwell Shimba
Shimba Theological Institute

DR. MAXWELL SHIMBA

CHAPTER 01

INTRODUCTION TO RESTORATIVE JUSTICE

Restorative justice is an innovative approach to justice that seeks to repair the harm caused by criminal behavior through inclusive and cooperative processes involving all stakeholders. Unlike traditional punitive systems that focus on punishment and retribution, restorative justice emphasizes healing, accountability, and addressing the needs of victims, offenders, and the community.

What are Restorative Justice Circles?

Restorative justice circles are a structured, facilitated dialogue process that brings together those affected by a particular incident of harm—typically victims, offenders, and community members. The circle provides a safe and respectful space where participants can share their experiences, express their emotions, and collaboratively seek solutions to repair the harm.

The process is characterized by the following key elements:

- Inclusivity: All parties affected by the harm have an opportunity to participate and share their perspectives.

- Equality: Every participant's voice is valued equally, promoting a sense of respect and mutual understanding.

- Voluntariness: Participation in the circle is voluntary, ensuring that all involved are willing to engage in the process.

- Accountability: Offenders are encouraged to take responsibility for their actions and understand the impact of their behavior on others.

- Reparation: The goal is to identify ways to repair the harm caused, which may include apologies, restitution, or community service.

- Reintegration: The process supports the reintegration of offenders into the community, fostering a sense of belonging and reducing recidivism.

Where Can We Find Restorative Justice Circles?

Restorative justice circles can be found in a variety of settings, each adapting the process to meet specific needs and contexts. Some common environments where restorative justice circles are implemented include:

1. Schools: Many schools use restorative justice circles to address conflicts, bullying, and disciplinary issues. These circles help build a positive school culture, improve student behavior, and create a supportive environment for learning.

2. Workplaces: In professional settings, restorative justice circles are used to resolve disputes, improve communication, and foster a collaborative work culture. They can address issues such as harassment, discrimination, and conflicts among employees.

3. Criminal Justice System: Restorative justice circles are increasingly used as an alternative to traditional court proceedings for certain offenses. They provide a platform for victims to voice their experiences, for offenders to take responsibility, and for communities to participate in the justice process.

4. Communities: Local communities use restorative justice circles to address various issues, including neighborhood disputes, vandalism, and other forms of misconduct. These circles strengthen community bonds and promote collective problem-solving.

5. Family and Youth Services: Organizations working with families and youth often use restorative justice circles to address conflicts, improve relationships, and support at-risk youth in making positive changes.

Who Arranges the Circles?

The organization and facilitation of restorative justice circles typically involve trained facilitators who guide the process and ensure a safe and respectful environment. Facilitators play a crucial role in maintaining the structure and flow of the circle, encouraging open dialogue, and helping participants reach a consensus on how to repair the harm. The facilitators may come from various backgrounds, including:

1. Community Organizations: Local non-profits, community centers, and advocacy groups often have trained facilitators who organize and lead restorative justice circles within their communities.

2. Schools: In educational settings, teachers, counselors, or dedicated restorative justice coordinators are often trained to facilitate circles. They work with students, staff, and parents to address conflicts and build a positive school culture.

3. Workplace Mediators: In professional environments, human resources personnel or trained workplace mediators may arrange and facilitate restorative justice circles to resolve conflicts and improve workplace dynamics.

4. Justice System Professionals: Within the criminal justice system, probation officers, social workers, or specially

trained restorative justice practitioners may organize and lead circles as part of diversion programs, alternative sentencing, or post-incarceration support.

5. Independent Practitioners: Some facilitators operate independently, offering their services to various organizations, schools, and communities. These practitioners often have specialized training and experience in restorative justice processes.

In all cases, the success of restorative justice circles relies on the skill and dedication of the facilitators, the willingness of participants to engage in the process, and the support of the broader community or organization in implementing restorative justice principles.

Conclusion

Restorative justice circles represent a powerful approach to addressing harm and fostering healing within communities. By emphasizing inclusivity, accountability, and reparation, these circles provide a meaningful alternative to traditional punitive systems, promoting understanding, empathy, and collective problem-solving. As the practice of restorative justice continues to grow and evolve, its potential to transform individuals and communities becomes increasingly evident.

Restorative justice circles are a specific application of restorative justice principles, where participants sit in a circle and engage in open dialogue to address harm, promote understanding, and seek collective resolutions. This chapter will explore the foundational concepts of restorative justice and the role of circles in fostering community healing.

Understanding Restorative Justice

Restorative justice is an approach to justice that emphasizes repairing the harm caused by criminal behavior through inclusive and cooperative processes involving all stakeholders. Unlike traditional punitive systems that focus on punishment and retribution, restorative justice emphasizes healing, accountability, and addressing the needs of victims, offenders, and the community. The main goals of restorative justice include:

- Healing for Victims: Providing victims with a platform to express their pain, ask questions, and receive restitution.

- Accountability for Offenders: Encouraging offenders to understand the impact of their actions and take responsibility.

- Community Involvement: Involving the community in the healing process and restoring trust.

What are Restorative Justice Circles?

Restorative justice circles are a structured, facilitated dialogue process that brings together those affected by a particular incident of harm—typically victims, offenders, and community members. The circle provides a safe and respectful space where participants can share their experiences, express their emotions, and collaboratively seek solutions to repair the harm.

Key Elements of Restorative Justice Circles

1. Inclusivity: All parties affected by the harm have an opportunity to participate and share their perspectives.

2. Equality: Every participant's voice is valued equally, promoting a sense of respect and mutual understanding.

3. Voluntariness: Participation in the circle is voluntary, ensuring that all involved are willing to engage in the process.

4. Accountability: Offenders are encouraged to take responsibility for their actions and understand the impact of their behavior on others.

5. Reparation: The goal is to identify ways to repair the harm caused, which may include apologies, restitution, or community service.

6. Reintegration: The process supports the reintegration of offenders into the community, fostering a sense of belonging and reducing recidivism.

The Role of Circles in Fostering Community Healing

Restorative justice circles play a crucial role in fostering community healing by providing a space for dialogue, understanding, and collective problem-solving. Here's how they contribute to healing:

1. Empowerment of Victims: Circles give victims a voice and an active role in the justice process, helping them regain a sense of control and closure.

2. Offender Accountability: By facing their victims and hearing about the impact of their actions, offenders are more likely to take genuine responsibility and make amends.

3. Community Strengthening: Involving community members in the process helps rebuild trust, reinforce social norms, and promote collective responsibility.

4. Preventing Recidivism: The supportive environment of a circle helps offenders feel valued and supported, reducing the likelihood of reoffending.

5. Promoting Understanding: Open dialogue promotes empathy and understanding among participants, fostering a sense of shared humanity and reducing conflict.

The Circle Process: Steps and Procedures

The circle process involves several key steps to ensure a structured and effective dialogue:

1. Preparation: Facilitators meet with participants individually to explain the process, address concerns, and ensure readiness for the circle.

2. Opening: The circle begins with a welcoming statement or ritual that sets a positive tone and establishes the purpose of the meeting.

3. Sharing: Participants take turns speaking, following established guidelines, and using a talking piece to ensure everyone has an equal opportunity to share.

4. Discussion: The group engages in a deeper dialogue to explore the harm, its impact, and possible resolutions. This step focuses on listening, empathy, and understanding.

5. Agreement: Participants work together to reach a consensus on how to repair the harm and prevent future occurrences. This may involve apologies, restitution, or community service.

6. Closing: The circle concludes with reflections and a closing ritual, reinforcing the commitments made and the collective effort toward healing.

Case Studies: Success Stories from Restorative Justice Circles

Real-world examples demonstrate the effectiveness of restorative justice circles. This section presents case studies from various settings, showcasing the transformative impact of this approach on individuals and communities.

Case Study 1: School Setting

In a middle school, a restorative justice circle was used to address a bullying incident. The circle included the victim, the offender, their parents, teachers, and a trained facilitator. Through the circle process, the victim expressed their feelings and the impact of the bullying. The offender took responsibility, apologized, and committed to positive behavior changes. The community agreed on a plan to support both students, resulting in a safer and more supportive school environment.

Case Study 2: Community Setting

In a small town, a restorative justice circle was organized to address vandalism that had damaged public property. The circle included the young offenders, community members, and local officials. Through open dialogue, the offenders understood the broader impact of their actions on the community. They agreed to repair the damage and participate in community service projects. The process strengthened community bonds and helped the offenders reintegrate positively.

Challenges and Solutions in Restorative Justice Circles

While restorative justice circles can be highly effective, they also present challenges. This section identifies common obstacles, such as resistance from participants or cultural barriers, and offers strategies for overcoming them.

Common Challenges

- Resistance to Participation: Some individuals may be reluctant to participate due to fear, mistrust, or skepticism.

- Power Imbalances: Ensuring equal participation can be difficult when there are significant power imbalances among participants.

- Emotional Intensity: The process can be emotionally intense, requiring skilled facilitation to manage emotions and maintain a respectful environment.

Solutions

- Building Trust: Facilitators can build trust through thorough preparation, clear communication, and demonstrating empathy and respect.

- Training Facilitators: Providing comprehensive training for facilitators ensures they are equipped to manage the circle process effectively.

- Support Systems: Establishing support systems for participants, such as counseling or follow-up meetings, helps address ongoing emotional needs.

Conclusion

Restorative justice circles represent a powerful approach to addressing harm and fostering healing within communities. By emphasizing inclusivity, accountability, and reparation, these circles provide a meaningful alternative to traditional punitive systems, promoting understanding, empathy, and collective problem-solving. As the practice of restorative justice continues to grow and evolve, its potential to transform individuals and communities becomes increasingly evident.

This chapter has introduced the foundational concepts of restorative justice and the specific role of circles in fostering community healing. Subsequent chapters will delve deeper into the principles, implementation, and impact of restorative justice circles, providing practical insights and inspiration for those interested in adopting this transformative approach to justice.

Introduction to Restorative Justice Circles

Restorative justice circles are a specific application of restorative justice principles, where participants sit in a circle and engage in open dialogue to address harm, promote understanding, and seek collective resolutions. This chapter will explore the foundational concepts of restorative justice, the role of circles in fostering community healing, and how offenders and victims can benefit from these circles.

Understanding Restorative Justice

Restorative justice is an approach to justice that emphasizes repairing the harm caused by criminal behavior through inclusive and cooperative processes involving all stakeholders. Unlike traditional punitive systems that focus on punishment and retribution, restorative justice emphasizes healing, accountability, and addressing the needs of victims, offenders, and the community. The main goals of restorative justice include:

- Healing for Victims: Providing victims with a platform to express their pain, ask questions, and receive restitution.

- Accountability for Offenders: Encouraging offenders to understand the impact of their actions and take responsibility.

- Community Involvement: Involving the community in the healing process and restoring trust.

What are Restorative Justice Circles?

Restorative justice circles are a structured, facilitated dialogue process that brings together those affected by a particular incident of harm—typically victims, offenders, and community members. The circle provides a safe and respectful space where participants can share their experiences, express their emotions, and collaboratively seek solutions to repair the harm.

Key Elements of Restorative Justice Circles

1. Inclusivity: All parties affected by the harm have an opportunity to participate and share their perspectives.

2. Equality: Every participant's voice is valued equally, promoting a sense of respect and mutual understanding.

3. Voluntariness: Participation in the circle is voluntary, ensuring that all involved are willing to engage in the process.

4. Accountability: Offenders are encouraged to take responsibility for their actions and understand the impact of their behavior on others.

5. Reparation: The goal is to identify ways to repair the harm caused, which may include apologies, restitution, or community service.

6. Reintegration: The process supports the reintegration of offenders into the community, fostering a sense of belonging and reducing recidivism.

Benefits for Victims

Victims of crime often experience a range of emotions, including anger, fear, and a sense of helplessness. Traditional justice systems may not address these emotional needs effectively. Restorative justice circles offer several benefits for victims:

1. Voice and Empowerment: Victims are given the opportunity to tell their story, express their feelings, and be heard. This can be a powerful step towards healing and regaining a sense of control.

2. Understanding and Closure: The open dialogue allows victims to ask questions and receive answers directly from the offender, providing a deeper understanding of the incident and its context.

3. Emotional Healing: The process of sharing their experience and being acknowledged can be therapeutic, helping victims to process their emotions and begin to heal.

4. Restitution and Reparation: Victims can participate in deciding how the harm will be repaired, whether through apologies, financial restitution, or community service, ensuring that their needs are addressed.

5. Sense of Justice: Restorative justice provides a sense of justice that is more personal and meaningful, focusing on repair and reconciliation rather than punishment.

Benefits for Offenders

Offenders can also experience significant benefits from participating in restorative justice circles. This process can lead to personal growth, accountability, and positive behavioral changes:

1. Understanding Impact: Offenders are confronted with the human impact of their actions, which can lead to a greater understanding and empathy for their victims.

2. Taking Responsibility: The circle process encourages offenders to take responsibility for their actions, promoting a sense of accountability and moral development.

3. Rehabilitation and Reintegration: Participating in restorative justice circles can help offenders reintegrate into their community by repairing relationships and building trust.

4. Supportive Environment: The circle provides a supportive environment where offenders can express their feelings, seek forgiveness, and make amends.

5. Reduction in Recidivism: Studies have shown that offenders who participate in restorative justice programs are less likely to re-offend, as they develop a stronger sense of community and personal responsibility.

The Role of Circles in Fostering Community Healing

Restorative justice circles play a crucial role in fostering community healing by providing a space for dialogue, understanding, and collective problem-solving. Here's how they contribute to healing:

1. Empowerment of Victims: Circles give victims a voice and an active role in the justice process, helping them regain a sense of control and closure.

2. Offender Accountability: By facing their victims and hearing about the impact of their actions, offenders are more likely to take genuine responsibility and make amends.

3. Community Strengthening: Involving community members in the process helps rebuild trust, reinforce social norms, and promote collective responsibility.

4. Preventing Recidivism: The supportive environment of a circle helps offenders feel valued and supported, reducing the likelihood of reoffending.

5. Promoting Understanding: Open dialogue promotes empathy and understanding among participants, fostering a sense of shared humanity and reducing conflict.

The Circle Process: Steps and Procedures

The circle process involves several key steps to ensure a structured and effective dialogue:

1. Preparation: Facilitators meet with participants individually to explain the process, address concerns, and ensure readiness for the circle.

2. Opening: The circle begins with a welcoming statement or ritual that sets a positive tone and establishes the purpose of the meeting.

3. Sharing: Participants take turns speaking, following established guidelines, and using a talking piece to ensure everyone has an equal opportunity to share.

4. Discussion: The group engages in a deeper dialogue to explore the harm, its impact, and possible resolutions. This step focuses on listening, empathy, and understanding.

5. Agreement: Participants work together to reach a consensus on how to repair the harm and prevent future occurrences. This may involve apologies, restitution, or community service.

6. Closing: The circle concludes with reflections and a closing ritual, reinforcing the commitments made and the collective effort toward healing.

Case Studies: Success Stories from Restorative Justice Circles

Real-world examples demonstrate the effectiveness of restorative justice circles. This section presents case studies from various settings, showcasing the transformative impact of this approach on individuals and communities.

Case Study 1: School Setting

In a middle school, a restorative justice circle was used to address a bullying incident. The circle included the victim, the offender, their parents, teachers, and a trained facilitator. Through the circle process, the victim expressed their feelings and the impact of the bullying. The offender took responsibility, apologized, and committed to positive behavior changes. The community agreed on a plan to support both students, resulting in a safer and more supportive school environment.

Case Study 2: Community Setting

In a small town, a restorative justice circle was organized to address vandalism that had damaged public property. The circle included the young offenders, community members, and local officials. Through open dialogue, the offenders understood the broader impact of their actions on the community. They agreed to repair the damage and participate in community service projects. The process strengthened community bonds and helped the offenders reintegrate positively.

Challenges and Solutions in Restorative Justice Circles

While restorative justice circles can be highly effective, they also present challenges. This section identifies common obstacles, such as resistance from participants or cultural barriers, and offers strategies for overcoming them.

Common Challenges

- Resistance to Participation: Some individuals may be reluctant to participate due to fear, mistrust, or skepticism.

- Power Imbalances: Ensuring equal participation can be difficult when there are significant power imbalances among participants.

- Emotional Intensity: The process can be emotionally intense, requiring skilled facilitation to manage emotions and maintain a respectful environment.

Solutions

- Building Trust: Facilitators can build trust through thorough preparation, clear communication, and demonstrating empathy and respect.

- Training Facilitators: Providing comprehensive training for facilitators ensures they are equipped to manage the circle process effectively.

- Support Systems: Establishing support systems for participants, such as counseling or follow-up meetings, helps address ongoing emotional needs.

Conclusion

Restorative justice circles represent a powerful approach to addressing harm and fostering healing within communities. By emphasizing inclusivity, accountability, and reparation, these circles provide a meaningful alternative to traditional punitive systems, promoting understanding, empathy, and collective problem-solving. As the practice of restorative justice continues to grow and evolve, its potential to transform individuals and communities becomes increasingly evident.

This chapter has introduced the foundational concepts of restorative justice, the role of circles in fostering community healing, and the specific benefits for both victims and offenders. Subsequent chapters will delve deeper into the principles, implementation, and impact of restorative justice circles, providing practical insights and inspiration for those interested in adopting this transformative approach to justice.

CHAPTER 02

THE PRINCIPLES OF RESTORATIVE JUSTICE CIRCLES

Inclusivity in Restorative Justice Circles

Inclusivity is a foundational principle of restorative justice circles, essential for creating a space where healing and understanding can occur. Inclusivity ensures that all affected parties, including victims, offenders, and community members, are encouraged to participate and share their perspectives. This chapter delves into the concept of inclusivity, its importance, and how it is implemented in restorative justice circles.

Understanding Inclusivity

Inclusivity in restorative justice circles means that every person impacted by the harm has the opportunity to be involved in the process. This broad participation is crucial because it:

1. Ensures Comprehensive Perspectives: By involving all affected parties, a fuller picture of the incident and its impact emerges.

2. Promotes Empathy and Understanding: Hearing diverse viewpoints fosters empathy among participants, helping them understand the experiences and feelings of others.

3. Facilitates Collective Healing: When everyone affected by the harm is included, the process of healing and resolution becomes a communal effort, strengthening community bonds.

4. Empowers Participants: Giving all stakeholders a voice in the process empowers them to contribute to the resolution and healing, restoring a sense of agency and control.

The Role of Inclusivity in Restorative Justice Circles

Inclusivity in restorative justice circles involves several key components:

1. Identifying Affected Parties: This includes not just the direct victim and offender but also others who might be impacted, such as family members, friends, witnesses, and community members.

2. Creating a Safe Environment: Facilitators must ensure a safe and respectful space where all participants feel comfortable sharing their thoughts and feelings.

3. Encouraging Participation: Efforts are made to invite and encourage the participation of all affected parties, addressing any barriers that might prevent involvement.

4. Valuing Every Voice: All participants are given equal opportunities to speak and be heard, ensuring that no single perspective dominates the conversation.

Implementing Inclusivity in Restorative Justice Circles

To implement inclusivity effectively, facilitators and organizers must consider several strategies and practices:

1. Outreach and Engagement:

- Identifying Stakeholders: Carefully identifying who has been affected by the harm and reaching out to them personally.

- Building Trust: Establishing trust with potential participants through clear communication, empathy, and transparency about the process.

2. Facilitator Training:

- Skills Development: Training facilitators to recognize and address power imbalances, cultural differences, and communication barriers.

- Sensitivity: Ensuring facilitators are sensitive to the needs and concerns of all participants, fostering an inclusive atmosphere.

3. Creating Safe Spaces:

- Physical Environment: Choosing a neutral and comfortable location for the circle.

- Emotional Safety: Establishing ground rules that promote respect, confidentiality, and non-judgmental listening.

4. Encouraging Participation:

- Voluntary Involvement: Ensuring that participation is voluntary and that all parties understand their role and the benefits of the process.

- Support Systems: Providing support, such as counseling or legal advice, to participants who may need it.

5. Cultural Competence:

- Understanding Diversity: Recognizing and respecting the cultural backgrounds and values of participants.

- Adaptation: Adapting the circle process to accommodate cultural practices and norms.

Benefits of Inclusivity

Inclusivity in restorative justice circles brings numerous benefits to the process and its participants:

1. Enhanced Understanding: When all voices are heard, participants gain a more comprehensive understanding of the incident and its impact.

2. Greater Empathy: Hearing different perspectives fosters empathy and compassion among participants, which is crucial for healing and reconciliation.

3. Empowerment: Inclusive participation empowers victims, offenders, and community members by giving them a stake in the resolution process.

4. Strengthened Community: Inclusivity helps to rebuild trust and strengthen relationships within the community, creating a supportive network for the future.

5. Sustainable Solutions: Solutions that emerge from an inclusive process are more likely to be effective and sustainable, as they reflect the needs and perspectives of all affected parties.

Challenges to Inclusivity and How to Overcome Them

While inclusivity is vital, it can also present challenges. Some common obstacles and strategies to address them include:

1. Resistance to Participation:

- Overcoming Fear and Mistrust: Building trust through transparency, empathy, and providing clear information about the process.

- Support and Encouragement: Offering support to participants who may be hesitant, such as providing emotional or logistical assistance.

2. Power Imbalances:

- Facilitator Intervention: Facilitators can actively manage discussions to ensure that all voices are heard and that no single participant dominates.

- Equal Opportunities: Establishing clear guidelines for equal participation, such as using a talking piece to manage speaking turns.

3. Cultural and Language Barriers:

- Cultural Sensitivity Training: Training facilitators to be aware of and sensitive to cultural differences.

- Translation and Interpretation: Providing translation or interpretation services to ensure that language barriers do not impede participation.

4. Logistical Issues:

- Accessibility: Ensuring that the location of the circle is accessible to all participants.

- Scheduling Flexibility: Scheduling meetings at times that are convenient for all parties, considering their availability and commitments.

Conclusion

Inclusivity is a cornerstone of restorative justice circles, ensuring that all affected parties are involved in the process of addressing harm, promoting understanding, and seeking collective resolutions. By valuing every voice and fostering an environment of respect and equality, restorative justice circles can achieve meaningful healing and reconciliation. Implementing inclusivity requires careful planning, skilled facilitation, and a commitment to creating a safe and supportive space for all participants.

As we continue to explore the principles of restorative justice circles in subsequent chapters, the importance of inclusivity will remain a central theme, underscoring its role in building stronger, more resilient communities.

The Principles of Restorative Justice Circles

Voluntariness in Restorative Justice Circles

Voluntariness is a fundamental principle of restorative justice circles, ensuring that participation is entirely voluntary for all parties involved. This chapter explores the concept of voluntariness, its importance, and how it is implemented in restorative justice circles.

Understanding Voluntariness

Voluntariness means that no one is compelled to participate in the restorative justice circle. All participants, including victims, offenders, and community members, must choose to engage in the process willingly. This principle is crucial for several reasons:

1. Respect for Autonomy: Respecting each individual's autonomy and right to make their own decisions fosters a sense of dignity and respect.

2. Genuine Engagement: Voluntary participation ensures that individuals are genuinely engaged and committed to the process, enhancing its effectiveness.

3. Trust and Safety: Knowing that participation is voluntary helps build trust and a sense of safety among participants.

The Role of Voluntariness in Restorative Justice Circles

Voluntariness plays a critical role in the success of restorative justice circles by ensuring that the process is collaborative and consensual. Key aspects of voluntariness include:

1. Informed Consent: Participants must fully understand the process, their roles, and the potential outcomes before agreeing to participate.

2. Freedom to Withdraw: Participants should feel free to withdraw from the process at any time without facing negative consequences.

3. No Coercion: There should be no coercion, pressure, or undue influence on individuals to participate in the circle.

Implementing Voluntariness in Restorative Justice Circles

To implement voluntariness effectively, facilitators and organizers must adopt several strategies and practices:

1. Providing Clear Information:

- Explanation of the Process: Clearly explain the restorative justice circle process, including its purpose, structure, and potential outcomes.

- Roles and Responsibilities: Ensure that participants understand their roles and responsibilities within the circle.

2. Informed Consent:

- Consent Forms: Use consent forms to document participants' understanding and agreement to participate.

- Opportunity for Questions: Allow participants to ask questions and seek clarification before giving their consent.

3. Ensuring Freedom to Withdraw:

- Open Communication: Communicate clearly that participants can withdraw from the process at any time.

- Support Systems: Provide support, such as counseling or legal advice, for participants who may be considering withdrawal.

4. Avoiding Coercion:

- Neutral Presentation: Present the restorative justice circle as one of several options, without implying that it is the only or best choice.

- Independent Decision-Making: Encourage participants to make their decision independently, without pressure from facilitators or others.

Benefits of Voluntariness

Voluntariness in restorative justice circles brings several benefits to the process and its participants:

1. Enhanced Commitment: Voluntary participation ensures that individuals are committed to the process, leading to more meaningful and constructive engagement.

2. Genuine Accountability: Offenders who choose to participate are more likely to take genuine responsibility for their actions and make sincere efforts to repair the harm.

3. Respect for Participants: Voluntariness demonstrates respect for participants' autonomy and dignity, fostering a positive and respectful environment.

4. Trust and Safety: Knowing that participation is voluntary helps build trust among participants, creating a safe space for open and honest dialogue.

Challenges to Voluntariness and How to Overcome Them

While voluntariness is essential, it can also present challenges. Some common obstacles and strategies to address them include:

1. Lack of Information:

- Comprehensive Education: Provide comprehensive education about the restorative justice process to ensure participants are fully informed.

- Clear Communication: Use clear and straightforward language to explain the process, avoiding jargon or technical terms.

2. Fear of Consequences:

- Reassurance: Reassure participants that their decision to participate or withdraw will not result in negative consequences.

- Confidentiality: Emphasize the confidentiality of the process to alleviate fears about sharing personal information.

3. Pressure from Others:

- Independent Decision-Making: Encourage participants to make their decision independently, without influence from family members, friends, or authorities.

- Support Networks: Offer access to independent support networks, such as counselors or advisors, to help participants make informed decisions.

4. Misunderstanding Voluntariness:

- Ongoing Clarification: Continuously clarify the voluntary nature of the process throughout the preparation and participation stages.

- Regular Check-Ins: Conduct regular check-ins with participants to ensure they still feel comfortable and willing to continue.

Case Studies Highlighting Voluntariness

Case Study 1: Voluntariness in a School Setting

In a high school, a restorative justice circle was proposed to address a fight between two students. The facilitators ensured that both students and their parents fully understood the process and could freely decide whether to participate. One student initially hesitated but, after discussing the process with a school counselor and understanding its voluntary nature, chose to participate. The circle resulted in both students taking responsibility and apologizing, leading to a significant reduction in tension and improved relationships within the school.

Case Study 2: Voluntariness in a Community Setting

In a neighborhood dispute involving property damage, a restorative justice circle was organized. The facilitators met with the involved parties individually, explaining the voluntary nature of the process and addressing their concerns. One homeowner was initially skeptical but decided to participate after being assured that they could withdraw at any time. The circle facilitated open dialogue, leading to mutual understanding and an agreement on restitution, which strengthened community ties.

Conclusion

Voluntariness is a cornerstone of restorative justice circles, ensuring that participation is based on informed and free choice. By respecting each individual's autonomy and fostering a sense of genuine engagement, voluntariness enhances the effectiveness of the restorative justice process. Implementing voluntariness requires clear communication, informed consent, and a commitment to avoiding coercion.

As we continue to explore the principles of restorative justice circles in subsequent chapters, the importance of voluntariness will remain a central theme, underscoring its role in creating a respectful, trustworthy, and effective process for addressing harm and fostering healing.

The Principles of Restorative Justice Circles

Respect and Equality in Restorative Justice Circles

Respect and equality are fundamental principles of restorative justice circles, ensuring that every participant's voice is valued equally. This chapter explores the concepts of respect and equality, their importance in restorative justice circles, and how they are implemented to foster an environment of mutual understanding and healing.

Understanding Respect and Equality

Respect and equality in restorative justice circles mean recognizing and valuing the inherent worth of each participant, regardless of their role or perspective. These principles ensure that:

1. Every Voice is Heard: Each participant has an equal opportunity to speak and be heard without interruption or prejudice.

2. Mutual Respect: Participants treat each other with dignity and consideration, acknowledging each person's experiences and feelings.

3. Equal Participation: All participants have an equal role in the process, with no single voice dominating the discussion.

The Role of Respect and Equality in Restorative Justice Circles

Respect and equality are crucial for creating a safe and constructive environment in restorative justice circles. Key aspects include:

1. Creating a Safe Space: Ensuring that the circle is a safe and respectful space where participants feel comfortable sharing their thoughts and emotions.

2. Facilitator's Role: The facilitator plays a vital role in modeling and maintaining respect and equality throughout the process.

3. Balancing Power Dynamics: Addressing and managing any power imbalances to ensure that all voices are equally valued.

Implementing Respect and Equality in Restorative Justice Circles

To implement respect and equality effectively, facilitators and organizers must adopt several strategies and practices:

1. Establishing Ground Rules:

- Clear Guidelines: Setting clear guidelines at the beginning of the circle to promote respectful communication and equal participation.

- Shared Agreement: Having all participants agree to the ground rules to ensure a collective commitment to respect and equality.

2. Facilitator Training:

- Modeling Respect: Training facilitators to model respectful behavior and to intervene if disrespect occurs.

- Managing Discussions: Equipping facilitators with skills to manage discussions, ensuring that everyone has an opportunity to speak.

3. Using a Talking Piece:

- Equal Turn-Taking: Implementing the use of a talking piece, which is passed around the circle to ensure that only the person holding it speaks, promoting equal turn-taking.

- Focused Listening: Encouraging participants to listen attentively and without interruption when others are speaking.

4. Encouraging Full Participation:

- Inviting Contributions: Actively inviting contributions from all participants, especially those who may be quieter or hesitant to speak.

- Addressing Imbalances: Being mindful of and addressing any power imbalances, ensuring that marginalized voices are heard and valued.

5. Creating an Inclusive Environment:

- Cultural Sensitivity: Recognizing and respecting cultural differences, adapting the process to be inclusive of diverse backgrounds.

- Accessibility: Ensuring that the circle is accessible to all participants, considering physical, linguistic, and other potential barriers.

Benefits of Respect and Equality

Respect and equality in restorative justice circles bring numerous benefits to the process and its participants:

1. Enhanced Trust: When participants feel respected and valued, it builds trust in the process and among each other.

2. Open Dialogue: Respectful and equal participation fosters open and honest dialogue, essential for understanding and healing.

3. Empowerment: Valuing each voice equally empowers participants, giving them confidence and a sense of agency in the process.

4. Mutual Understanding: Respectful listening and equal participation promote mutual understanding, reducing conflict and fostering empathy.

5. Sustainable Solutions: Solutions that emerge from a respectful and equal process are more likely to be effective

and sustainable, as they reflect the needs and perspectives of all participants.

Challenges to Respect and Equality and How to Overcome Them

While respect and equality are essential, they can also present challenges. Some common obstacles and strategies to address them include:

1. Dominating Voices:

- Facilitator Intervention: Facilitators can intervene to ensure that no single participant dominates the discussion, encouraging equal participation.

- Structured Turn-Taking: Implementing structured turn-taking mechanisms, such as the talking piece, to manage contributions.

2. Cultural and Language Barriers:

- Cultural Competence: Training facilitators to be culturally competent, recognizing and respecting diverse communication styles and values.

- Translation Services: Providing translation or interpretation services to ensure that language barriers do not impede participation.

3. Power Imbalances:

- Addressing Power Dynamics: Being aware of and actively addressing power dynamics within the circle, ensuring that marginalized voices are heard.

- Equal Opportunities: Creating opportunities for all participants to contribute equally, regardless of their status or role.

4. Emotional Intensity:

- Emotional Support: Providing emotional support and resources for participants who may struggle with the emotional intensity of the process.

- Safe Space: Ensuring that the circle remains a safe and respectful space, where participants can express their emotions without fear of judgment.

Case Studies Highlighting Respect and Equality

Case Study 1: Respect and Equality in a School Setting

In a high school, a restorative justice circle was used to address a conflict between several students. The facilitator established ground rules that emphasized respect and equality, using a talking piece to ensure that each student had an equal opportunity to speak. The respectful environment allowed the students to share their perspectives and feelings openly, leading to a mutual understanding and a collective resolution. The process not only resolved the conflict but also strengthened relationships within the school.

Case Study 2: Respect and Equality in a Community Setting

In a community affected by a series of vandalism incidents, a restorative justice circle was organized to address the harm. The circle included the offenders, victims, and community members. The facilitator emphasized respect and equality, ensuring that all voices were heard and valued. The open and respectful dialogue helped the offenders understand the impact of their actions and led to a community agreement on restitution and future prevention measures. The process fostered a sense of community and collective responsibility.

Conclusion

Respect and equality are cornerstones of restorative justice circles, ensuring that every participant's voice is valued equally. By fostering an environment of mutual respect and equal participation, restorative justice circles can achieve meaningful healing and reconciliation. Implementing respect and equality requires clear guidelines, skilled facilitation, and a commitment to creating a safe and inclusive space for all participants.

As we continue to explore the principles of restorative justice circles in subsequent chapters, the importance of respect and equality will remain a central theme, underscoring their role in creating a respectful, trustworthy, and effective process for addressing harm and fostering healing.

Accountability in Restorative Justice Circles

Accountability is a crucial principle in restorative justice circles, emphasizing that offenders must take responsibility for their actions. This chapter delves into the concept of accountability, its importance in restorative justice circles, and how it is implemented to facilitate healing and reconciliation.

Understanding Accountability

Accountability in restorative justice means that offenders acknowledge the harm they have caused, understand its impact, and take concrete steps to make amends. This principle is vital because:

1. Promotes Responsibility: Encourages offenders to take ownership of their actions and their consequences.

2. Fosters Empathy: Helps offenders develop empathy by understanding the impact of their behavior on others.

3. Facilitates Healing: Provides victims with a sense of justice and closure, knowing that the offender has taken responsibility.

4. Encourages Behavioral Change: Supports the offender in making positive changes to prevent future harm.

The Role of Accountability in Restorative Justice Circles

Accountability plays a pivotal role in the restorative justice process by ensuring that offenders actively participate in repairing the harm they have caused. Key aspects of accountability include:

1. Acknowledgement of Harm: Offenders must recognize and admit the harm they have caused to the victim and the community.

2. Expression of Remorse: Offenders should express genuine remorse for their actions, demonstrating understanding and empathy.

3. Making Amends: Offenders are required to take concrete steps to repair the harm, which may include apologies, restitution, or community service.

4. Commitment to Change: Offenders should commit to behavioral changes to prevent future harm and reintegrate positively into the community.

Implementing Accountability in Restorative Justice Circles

To implement accountability effectively, facilitators and organizers must adopt several strategies and practices:

1. Preparation and Education:

- Understanding Accountability: Educate offenders about the importance of accountability and what it entails.

- Preparation Meetings: Hold individual preparation meetings with offenders to ensure they understand their role and expectations.

2. Facilitating Acknowledgement:

- Guided Discussions: Use guided discussions to help offenders articulate the harm they have caused and its impact on others.

- Reflective Questions: Ask reflective questions that prompt offenders to think deeply about their actions and their consequences.

3. Encouraging Remorse:

- Empathy Building: Facilitate empathy-building exercises that help offenders connect with the victim's experience.

- Open Dialogue: Provide a safe space for offenders to express their feelings and remorse.

4. Supporting Amends:

- Action Plans: Develop action plans with offenders that outline specific steps they will take to make amends.

- Restitution Agreements: Facilitate agreements on restitution or other forms of reparation, ensuring they are realistic and achievable.

5. Promoting Behavioral Change:

- Support Systems: Provide access to support systems, such as counseling or mentorship, to help offenders make positive changes.

- Ongoing Monitoring: Implement mechanisms for ongoing monitoring and support to ensure that offenders follow through on their commitments.

Benefits of Accountability

Accountability in restorative justice circles brings numerous benefits to the process and its participants:

1. Victim Empowerment: Victims feel empowered and validated when offenders acknowledge the harm and take responsibility.

2. Offender Rehabilitation: Offenders gain a deeper understanding of the impact of their actions, fostering personal growth and rehabilitation.

3. Community Healing: The community benefits from a sense of justice and collective healing, knowing that the harm is being addressed constructively.

4. Prevention of Future Harm: Accountability helps prevent future harm by encouraging offenders to adopt positive behaviors and attitudes.

5. Strengthened Relationships: The process of making amends can help rebuild trust and strengthen relationships between victims, offenders, and the community.

Challenges to Accountability and How to Overcome Them

While accountability is essential, it can also present challenges. Some common obstacles and strategies to address them include:

1. Denial of Responsibility:

- Facilitated Reflection: Use facilitated reflection to help offenders understand and acknowledge their responsibility.

- Empathy Exercises: Engage offenders in empathy exercises to help them connect with the victim's experience.

2. Lack of Genuine Remorse:

- Building Understanding: Provide education and support to help offenders develop a deeper understanding of the impact of their actions.

- Creating Safe Spaces: Ensure a safe and non-judgmental space where offenders feel comfortable expressing their feelings.

3. Inadequate Reparation:

- Realistic Agreements: Facilitate realistic and achievable reparation agreements that reflect the harm caused.

- Support and Resources: Provide offenders with the support and resources needed to fulfill their reparation commitments.

4. Resistance to Behavioral Change:

- Ongoing Support: Offer ongoing support and mentorship to help offenders make and sustain positive changes.

- Accountability Mechanisms: Implement mechanisms for regular check-ins and accountability to ensure follow-through.

Case Studies Highlighting Accountability

Case Study 1: Accountability in a School Setting

In a high school, a restorative justice circle was used to address a case of theft. The offender, a student, initially denied responsibility. Through guided discussions and empathy-building exercises, the students came to understand the impact of their actions on the victim and the school community. The student expressed genuine remorse, apologized, and agreed to return the stolen items and perform community service. The process not only resolved the conflict but also led to positive behavioral changes in the student.

Case Study 2: Accountability in a Community Setting

In a neighborhood affected by vandalism, a restorative justice circle was organized. The offenders, a group of teenagers, initially showed little remorse. The facilitator used reflective questions and open dialogue to help the teenagers understand the broader impact of their actions. The teenagers acknowledged the harm, apologized to the affected community members, and agreed to repair the damage. They also participated in community service projects, fostering a sense of responsibility and commitment to positive change.

Conclusion

Accountability is a cornerstone of restorative justice circles, ensuring that offenders take responsibility for their actions and make amends for the harm caused. By fostering a sense of ownership, empathy, and commitment to change, accountability facilitates healing and reconciliation for victims, offenders, and the community. Implementing accountability requires careful preparation, guided discussions, and ongoing support to ensure that offenders understand their role and follow through on their commitments.

As we continue to explore the principles of restorative justice circles in subsequent chapters, the importance of accountability will remain a central theme, underscoring its role in creating a respectful, trustworthy, and effective process for addressing harm and fostering healing.

Reparation in Restorative Justice Circles

Reparation is a vital principle of restorative justice circles, focusing on making efforts to repair the harm caused to the victim and the community. This chapter delves into the concept of reparation, its importance in restorative justice circles, and how it is implemented to facilitate healing and reconciliation.

Understanding Reparation

Reparation in restorative justice involves taking tangible steps to address and mend the harm caused by the offender's actions. This principle is essential because:

1. Restores Balance: Reparation aims to restore balance by addressing the needs and losses of the victim and the community.

2. Fosters Healing: It provides a pathway for healing by acknowledging the harm and actively working to make things right.

3. Promotes Accountability: Offenders take responsibility for their actions by contributing to the repair of the damage they caused.

4. Rebuilds Trust: Through acts of reparation, trust can be rebuilt between the victim, the offender, and the community.

The Role of Reparation in Restorative Justice Circles

Reparation plays a pivotal role in the restorative justice process by ensuring that offenders actively participate in the healing process. Key aspects of reparation include:

1. Acknowledging Harm: Recognizing the harm caused and its impact on the victim and the community.

2. Taking Responsibility: Offenders take responsibility for their actions by agreeing to make amends.

3. Making Amends: Implementing specific actions to repair the harm, which can include apologies, restitution, or community service.

4. Ensuring Fairness: Ensuring that reparation efforts are fair, appropriate, and meaningful for all parties involved.

Implementing Reparation in Restorative Justice Circles

To implement reparation effectively, facilitators and organizers must adopt several strategies and practices:

1. Identifying Harm:

- Comprehensive Assessment: Conduct a thorough assessment to identify the harm caused to the victim and the community.

- Victim Input: Involve the victim in identifying their needs and what they consider appropriate reparation.

2. Developing Reparation Plans:

- Collaborative Planning: Work collaboratively with all parties to develop a reparation plan that addresses the identified harm.

- Realistic and Achievable Goals: Ensure that the reparation actions are realistic and achievable for the offender.

3. Facilitating Apologies:

- Sincere Apologies: Encourage offenders to offer sincere apologies to the victim, acknowledging the harm and expressing remorse.

- Structured Apologies: Provide guidance on how to structure apologies to ensure they are meaningful and respectful.

4. Restitution and Compensation:

- Financial Restitution: Facilitate financial restitution if the harm involves monetary loss, ensuring that it is fair and feasible.

- In-Kind Compensation: Explore options for in-kind compensation, such as providing services or goods to the victim.

5. Community Service:

- Service Projects: Develop community service projects that allow offenders to contribute positively to the community.

- Aligning Interests: Align community service activities with the interests and skills of the offender to ensure meaningful engagement.

6. Monitoring and Support:

- Ongoing Monitoring: Implement mechanisms for ongoing monitoring to ensure that reparation commitments are fulfilled.

- Support Systems: Provide support systems, such as counseling or mentorship, to help offenders complete their reparation obligations.

Benefits of Reparation

Reparation in restorative justice circles brings numerous benefits to the process and its participants:

1. Victim Empowerment: Victims feel empowered and validated when their needs are acknowledged and addressed.

2. Offender Accountability: Offenders learn to take responsibility for their actions by actively participating in making amends.

3. Community Healing: The community benefits from acts of reparation, which can restore trust and social harmony.

4. Preventing Recidivism: Engaging in reparation activities helps offenders develop a sense of responsibility and community connection, reducing the likelihood of reoffending.

5. Restored Relationships: The process of making amends can help restore relationships and foster a sense of forgiveness and reconciliation.

Challenges to Reparation and How to Overcome Them

While reparation is essential, it can also present challenges. Some common obstacles and strategies to address them include:

1. Resistance to Making Amends:

- Facilitated Discussions: Use facilitated discussions to help offenders understand the importance of making amends and the impact of their actions.

- Empathy Building: Engage offenders in empathy-building exercises to help them connect with the victim's experience.

2. Inadequate Resources:

- Realistic Planning: Ensure that reparation plans are realistic and consider the offender's resources and capabilities.

- Alternative Solutions: Explore alternative solutions for reparation, such as in-kind compensation or community service.

3. Disagreement on Reparation Terms:

- Mediation: Use mediation to resolve disagreements and reach a consensus on reparation terms that are fair to all parties.

- Flexibility: Be flexible and open to adjusting reparation plans to meet the needs and capacities of all participants.

4. Ensuring Follow-Through:

- Regular Check-Ins: Implement regular check-ins to monitor progress and provide support as needed.

- Accountability Measures: Establish accountability measures, such as written agreements or community oversight, to ensure follow-through.

Case Studies Highlighting Reparation

Case Study 1: Reparation in a School Setting

In a high school, a restorative justice circle was used to address a case of vandalism. The offender, a student, agreed to make amends by repairing the damaged property and offering a public apology to the school community. The reparation plan also included participating in a community service project related to school maintenance. The process helped the student understand the impact of their actions, take responsibility, and contribute positively to the school environment.

Case Study 2: Reparation in a Community Setting

In a community affected by a theft incident, a restorative justice circle was organized. The offender, a young adult, agreed to compensate the victim for the stolen items and participate in a community service project. The victim provided input on the reparation plan, which included both financial restitution and service activities that benefited the community. The process facilitated healing for the victim, accountability for the offender, and strengthened community bonds.

Conclusion

Reparation is a cornerstone of restorative justice circles, focusing on making efforts to repair the harm caused to the victim and the community. By emphasizing tangible actions to address the harm, reparation facilitates healing, accountability, and reconciliation. Implementing reparation requires careful planning, collaborative efforts, and ongoing support to ensure that the needs of all parties are met and that the process leads to meaningful outcomes.

As we continue to explore the principles of restorative justice circles in subsequent chapters, the importance of reparation will remain a central theme, underscoring its role in creating a respectful, trustworthy, and effective process for addressing harm and fostering healing.

Reintegration in Restorative Justice Circles

Reintegration is a fundamental principle of restorative justice circles, focusing on supporting offenders in rejoining the community as constructive members. This chapter explores the concept of reintegration, its importance in restorative justice circles, and how it is implemented to facilitate successful reintegration and community healing.

Understanding Reintegration

Reintegration involves helping offenders transition back into their communities after they have taken responsibility for their actions and made efforts to repair the harm they caused. This principle is essential because:

1. Promotes Social Inclusion: Reintegration prevents the marginalization and isolation of offenders by supporting their return to the community.

2. Reduces Recidivism: Providing support and resources for offenders helps reduce the likelihood of reoffending.

3. Fosters Community Healing: Successful reintegration contributes to the overall healing of the community by restoring relationships and trust.

4. Encourages Personal Growth: Reintegration supports offenders in making positive changes and developing a sense of belonging and purpose.

The Role of Reintegration in Restorative Justice Circles

Reintegration plays a pivotal role in the restorative justice process by ensuring that offenders are supported in their efforts to become constructive community members. Key aspects of reintegration include:

1. Creating Supportive Environments: Developing environments that support the offender's transition back into the community.

2. Providing Resources and Opportunities: Offering access to resources, education, and employment opportunities to facilitate successful reintegration.

3. Building Positive Relationships: Encouraging the development of positive relationships with community members, mentors, and support networks.

4. Monitoring and Guidance: Implementing ongoing monitoring and guidance to support the offender's progress and address any challenges.

Implementing Reintegration in Restorative Justice Circles

To implement reintegration effectively, facilitators and organizers must adopt several strategies and practices:

1. Developing Reintegration Plans:

- Collaborative Planning: Work collaboratively with offenders, victims, and community members to develop comprehensive reintegration plans.

- Individualized Plans: Tailor reintegration plans to meet the specific needs and circumstances of each offender.

2. Providing Access to Resources:

- Educational Opportunities: Offer access to educational programs and vocational training to enhance offenders' skills and employability.

- Employment Support: Provide support in finding and maintaining employment, such as job placement services and mentorship.

3. Facilitating Positive Relationships:

- Mentorship Programs: Establish mentorship programs that connect offenders with positive role models and support networks.

- Community Engagement: Encourage community engagement and participation in activities that promote social inclusion and positive interactions.

4. Offering Counseling and Support:

- Mental Health Services: Provide access to mental health services, including counseling and therapy, to address underlying issues and support personal growth.

- Substance Abuse Programs: Offer substance abuse programs and support for offenders dealing with addiction.

5. Implementing Monitoring and Guidance:

- Regular Check-Ins: Conduct regular check-ins to monitor progress and provide guidance as needed.

- Supportive Supervision: Implement supportive supervision that focuses on positive reinforcement and addressing challenges.

Benefits of Reintegration

Reintegration in restorative justice circles brings numerous benefits to the process and its participants:

1. Community Safety: Successful reintegration reduces the likelihood of reoffending, enhancing community safety.

2. Offender Rehabilitation: Offenders receive the support and resources needed to make positive changes and lead constructive lives.

3. Restored Relationships: Reintegration fosters the restoration of relationships between offenders, victims, and the community.

4. Social Cohesion: The process promotes social cohesion by preventing the marginalization and isolation of offenders.

5. Long-Term Healing: Reintegration contributes to long-term healing for all parties involved, as offenders become productive and valued members of the community.

Challenges to Reintegration and How to Overcome Them

While reintegration is essential, it can also present challenges. Some common obstacles and strategies to address them include:

1. Stigma and Discrimination:

- Community Education: Educate the community about the importance of reintegration and the potential for positive change in offenders.

- Anti-Discrimination Policies: Implement policies that protect offenders from discrimination in housing, employment, and other areas.

2. Lack of Resources:

- Resource Mobilization: Mobilize resources from various sectors, including government, non-profits, and the private sector, to support reintegration efforts.

- Partnerships: Develop partnerships with organizations that provide education, employment, and support services.

3. Resistance from Community Members:

- Community Involvement: Involve community members in the reintegration planning process to build understanding and support.

- Positive Role Models: Highlight success stories of offenders who have successfully reintegrated to demonstrate the potential for positive outcomes.

4. Offender Relapse:

- Ongoing Support: Provide ongoing support and supervision to help offenders navigate challenges and avoid relapse.

- Early Intervention: Implement early intervention strategies to address issues before they lead to relapse.

Case Studies Highlighting Reintegration

Case Study 1: Reintegration in a School Setting

In a high school, a restorative justice circle was used to address a case of bullying. The offender, a student, was supported in reintegrating into the school community through a comprehensive reintegration plan. The plan included counseling, participation in peer support groups, and involvement in positive extracurricular activities. With the support of teachers, counselors, and peers, the students successfully reintegrated, improved their behavior, and built positive relationships within the school.

Case Study 2: Reintegration in a Community Setting

In a community affected by theft, a restorative justice circle was organized. The offender, a young adult, was supported in reintegrating into the community through a tailored reintegration plan. The plan included vocational training, job placement assistance, and mentorship from community leaders. The offender also participated in community service projects, building positive connections with community members. The process facilitated successful reintegration, reduced recidivism, and strengthened community ties.

Conclusion

Reintegration is a cornerstone of restorative justice circles, focusing on supporting offenders in rejoining the community as constructive members. By emphasizing social inclusion, providing resources and support, and fostering positive relationships, reintegration facilitates successful transitions and long-term healing. Implementing reintegration requires careful planning, collaboration, and ongoing support to ensure that offenders have the tools and opportunities needed to lead constructive and fulfilling lives.

As we continue to explore the principles of restorative justice circles in subsequent chapters, the importance of reintegration will remain a central theme, underscoring its role in creating a respectful, trustworthy, and effective process for addressing harm and fostering healing.

CHAPTER 03

THE HISTORY AND EVOLUTION OF RESTORATIVE JUSTICE

Restorative justice has deep roots in indigenous cultures around the world, where community-based conflict resolution was the norm. This chapter traces the history and evolution of restorative justice, from its ancient origins to its modern-day applications. It also highlights key milestones and influential figures in the restorative justice movement.

Ancient Origins

Restorative justice principles have been practiced by various indigenous cultures for centuries, long before the term "restorative justice" was coined. These cultures often prioritized community harmony, reconciliation, and the restoration of relationships over punitive measures. Some examples include:

1. Maori of New Zealand: The Maori tradition of "Whakawhanaungatanga" emphasizes the importance of relationships and community connections. Disputes are resolved through a communal process that involves all affected parties, focusing on restoring harmony and balance.

2. First Nations of North America: Many First Nations communities in North America use "sentencing circles" or "healing circles" to address conflicts. These processes involve the victim, offender, and community members, aiming to heal the harm and restore relationships.

3. African Traditions: In various African cultures, restorative practices such as "Ubuntu" emphasize human interconnectedness and collective healing. Disputes are resolved through community gatherings where all voices are heard, and resolutions are sought collaboratively.

Medieval and Early Modern Periods

During the medieval and early modern periods, restorative principles were also evident in various justice systems:

1. English Common Law: Before the development of a centralized state justice system, English communities often relied on local, community-based methods of resolving disputes. The "hue and cry" system involved the entire community in apprehending offenders and addressing harm.

2. Continental Europe: In medieval Europe, many local communities used compensatory justice practices. Offenders were required to compensate victims directly, rather than being subjected to state-imposed punishments.

The Emergence of the Modern Justice System

With the rise of centralized states and the development of formal legal systems, the focus of justice shifted towards retribution and punishment. The modern justice system became more bureaucratic and less community-focused, emphasizing punishment over reconciliation.

The Revival of Restorative Justice

The modern restorative justice movement began to take shape in the mid-20th century as a response to the limitations of the retributive justice system. Key milestones and influential figures in the revival of restorative justice include:

1. Howard Zehr: Often referred to as the "grandfather of restorative justice," Zehr's 1990 book "Changing Lenses" played a pivotal role in shaping the modern restorative justice movement. Zehr emphasized the need to shift from a punitive to a restorative approach, focusing on healing rather than punishment.

2. The Mennonite Central Committee: In the 1970s, the Mennonite Central Committee in Canada initiated several

restorative justice programs, including victim-offender reconciliation programs (VORPs). These programs facilitated meetings between victims and offenders to discuss the harm and seek resolution.

3. New Zealand's Youth Justice System: In the late 1980s, New Zealand reformed its youth justice system to incorporate restorative principles. The Children, Young Persons, and Their Families Act of 1989 introduced family group conferences as an alternative to court proceedings for young offenders. This model has since influenced restorative justice practices worldwide.

Key Developments and Applications

Restorative justice has continued to evolve and expand, finding applications in various contexts:

1. Criminal Justice Systems: Many countries have incorporated restorative justice practices into their criminal justice systems. Programs such as victim-offender mediation, restorative justice conferences, and community service are used to address a wide range of offenses.

2. Educational Settings: Schools have adopted restorative practices to address bullying, conflicts, and disciplinary issues. Restorative circles and peer mediation programs promote a positive school culture and enhance student relationships.

3. Workplace and Organizational Contexts: Restorative practices are used in workplaces and organizations to resolve conflicts, improve communication, and foster a collaborative culture. These practices help address issues such as harassment, discrimination, and team disputes.

4. Community and Social Services: Community-based restorative justice programs address local issues such as neighborhood disputes, vandalism, and other forms of misconduct. These programs strengthen community bonds and promote collective problem-solving.

Influential Figures and Organizations

Several individuals and organizations have significantly contributed to the development and promotion of restorative justice:

1. Howard Zehr: As mentioned earlier, Zehr's work has been foundational in the modern restorative justice movement. His writings and teachings continue to influence practitioners and scholars.

2. Kay Pranis: A pioneer in the field, Pranis has written extensively on restorative practices and facilitated numerous training programs. Her work focuses on the importance of community involvement and the use of circles in restorative processes.

3. The Restorative Justice Council (RJC): Based in the UK, the RJC promotes restorative practices and provides resources, training, and accreditation for practitioners. The organization advocates for the integration of restorative justice into various sectors, including criminal justice, education, and social services.

4. The International Institute for Restorative Practices (IIRP): The IIRP is a global leader in restorative practices education and training. The institute offers graduate programs, professional development courses, and research initiatives to advance the field of restorative justice.

The Future of Restorative Justice

The restorative justice movement continues to grow and evolve, with increasing recognition of its potential to transform justice systems and communities. Future directions for restorative justice include:

1. Expanding Applications: Exploring new applications of restorative justice in areas such as environmental justice, healthcare, and corporate governance.

2. Integrating Technology: Utilizing technology to facilitate virtual restorative justice processes, making them more accessible and scalable.

3. Strengthening Evidence-Based Practice: Conducting rigorous research to evaluate the effectiveness of restorative justice practices and identify best practices.

4. Promoting Policy Change: Advocating for policy changes that support the implementation and sustainability of restorative justice programs at local, national, and international levels.

5. Building Inclusive Practices: Ensuring that restorative justice practices are inclusive and culturally sensitive, addressing the needs of diverse populations and marginalized communities.

Conclusion

The history and evolution of restorative justice reflect a deep-rooted tradition of community-based conflict resolution and healing. From its ancient origins in indigenous cultures to its modern-day applications, restorative justice has continually emphasized the importance of repairing harm, fostering accountability, and promoting reconciliation. As the movement continues to grow and evolve, its potential to transform justice systems and communities remains profound, offering a pathway toward a more just and compassionate world.

CHAPTER 04

IMPLEMENTING RESTORATIVE JUSTICE CIRCLES IN COMMUNITIES

Community Assessment: Understanding the Community's Needs and Readiness

Introducing restorative justice circles into a community requires a comprehensive understanding of the community's needs, dynamics, and readiness for such an initiative. A thorough community assessment is the first crucial step in implementing restorative justice circles effectively. This chapter explores the importance of community assessment, the steps involved, and the tools and strategies that can be used to gather and analyze relevant information.

The Importance of Community Assessment

A community assessment is essential for several reasons:

1. Identifies Needs and Issues: It helps identify the specific needs and issues within the community that restorative justice circles can address.

2. Gauges Readiness: It assesses the community's readiness and willingness to adopt restorative practices.

3. Informs Planning: It provides valuable information that informs the planning and implementation of restorative justice circles.

4. Builds Support: It helps build support and buy-in from community members and stakeholders.

5. Tailors Approaches: It ensures that restorative justice circles are tailored to the unique characteristics and dynamics of the community.

Steps in Conducting a Community Assessment

Conducting a community assessment involves several key steps:

1. Define the Scope and Objectives:

- Clarify Purpose: Clearly define the purpose of the assessment and the specific objectives you aim to achieve.

- Determine Scope: Determine the scope of the assessment, including the geographical area and the population to be studied.

2. Engage Stakeholders:

- Identify Key Stakeholders: Identify key stakeholders, including community leaders, local organizations, justice system representatives, and residents.

- Build Relationships: Build relationships with stakeholders to gain their support and involvement in the assessment process.

3. Collect Data:

- Use Multiple Methods: Use a variety of data collection methods to gather comprehensive information. These methods may include surveys, interviews, focus groups, community forums, and existing data analysis.

- Ensure Inclusivity: Ensure that data collection methods are inclusive and representative of the diverse voices within the community.

4. Analyze Data:

- Identify Themes and Patterns: Analyze the data to identify common themes, patterns, and key issues.

- Assess Readiness: Assess the community's readiness for restorative justice circles by evaluating factors such as awareness, attitudes, and existing support systems.

5. Report Findings:

- Prepare a Report: Prepare a comprehensive report that summarizes the findings of the assessment.

- Share with Stakeholders: Share the report with stakeholders and the broader community to ensure transparency and build collective understanding.

Tools and Strategies for Community Assessment

Several tools and strategies can be used to conduct a thorough community assessment:

1. Surveys and Questionnaires:

- Design and Distribution: Design surveys and questionnaires to gather quantitative data on community attitudes, awareness, and needs. Distribute them through various channels, such as online platforms, community centers, and local events.

- Analyze Responses: Analyze the responses to identify key trends and insights.

2. Interviews and Focus Groups:

- Conduct Interviews: Conduct one-on-one interviews with key stakeholders to gather in-depth qualitative data.

- Facilitate Focus Groups: Facilitate focus groups with different segments of the community to explore specific issues and gather diverse perspectives.

3. Community Forums and Public Meetings:

- Organize Forums: Organize community forums and public meetings to engage a broad audience in discussions about restorative justice and community needs.

- Encourage Participation: Encourage participation by promoting the events widely and creating a welcoming environment.

4. Asset Mapping:

- Identify Community Assets: Conduct asset mapping to identify the strengths, resources, and existing support systems within the community.

- Leverage Assets: Leverage these assets in the planning and implementation of restorative justice circles.

5. SWOT Analysis:

- Evaluate Strengths, Weaknesses, Opportunities, and Threats: Conduct a SWOT analysis to evaluate the community's strengths, weaknesses, opportunities, and threats related to implementing restorative justice circles.

Analyzing and Interpreting Data

Once data is collected, the next step is to analyze and interpret it to gain meaningful insights:

1. Categorize Data: Organize the data into categories based on common themes and issues.

2. Identify Key Issues: Identify key issues that restorative justice circles can address, such as conflict resolution, crime prevention, or community building.

3. Evaluate Readiness: Evaluate the community's readiness by assessing factors such as awareness of restorative justice, willingness to participate, and existing support structures.

4. Develop Recommendations: Develop recommendations based on the findings, outlining steps for implementing restorative justice circles and addressing identified needs.

Reporting and Sharing Findings

After analyzing the data, it is essential to report and share the findings with stakeholders and the community:

1. Prepare a Comprehensive Report: Prepare a detailed report that summarizes the assessment process, key findings, and recommendations.

2. Present to Stakeholders: Present the report to key stakeholders, including community leaders, local organizations, and justice system representatives.

3. Engage the Community: Share the findings with the broader community through public meetings, forums, and online platforms. Engage community members in discussions about the findings and next steps.

Building Support and Buy-In

Building support and buy-in from the community is crucial for the successful implementation of restorative justice circles:

1. Communicate Benefits: Clearly communicate the benefits of restorative justice circles to the community, emphasizing how they address identified needs and contribute to community well-being.

2. Involve Stakeholders: Involve stakeholders in the planning and implementation process, ensuring that their voices are heard and their input is valued.

3. Foster Collaboration: Foster collaboration between different sectors, such as education, law enforcement, social services, and community organizations, to create a supportive network for restorative justice initiatives.

Case Study: Community Assessment in Action

Case Study: Implementing Restorative Justice Circles in a Small Town

In a small town experiencing rising youth delinquency and community conflicts, a group of local leaders decided to explore the implementation of restorative justice circles. They began with a comprehensive community assessment to understand the needs and readiness of the town.

1. Engaging Stakeholders: The leaders identified key stakeholders, including school officials, law enforcement, youth organizations, and residents. They built relationships with these stakeholders and gained their support for the assessment process.

2. Collecting Data: The team used a combination of surveys, interviews, focus groups, and community forums to gather data. They ensured inclusivity by reaching out to diverse segments of the community, including marginalized groups.

3. Analyzing Data: The analysis revealed key issues such as a lack of constructive activities for youth, strained relationships between law enforcement and residents, and a general lack of awareness about restorative justice.

4. Developing Recommendations: Based on the findings, the team developed recommendations that included establishing restorative justice circles in schools, creating mentorship programs for youth, and organizing community education sessions on restorative practices.

5. Building Support: The findings and recommendations were shared with stakeholders and the community through public meetings and forums. The team engaged community members in discussions about the

benefits of restorative justice circles and how they could address the identified needs.

Conclusion

A thorough community assessment is a foundational step in implementing restorative justice circles. By understanding the community's needs, dynamics, and readiness, stakeholders can develop tailored and effective restorative justice initiatives. The assessment process involves engaging stakeholders, collecting and analyzing data, and building support and buy-in from the community. By taking these steps, communities can create a strong foundation for successful restorative justice circles that promote healing, accountability, and social cohesion.

Implementing Restorative Justice Circles in Communities

Building Partnerships: Engaging Stakeholders Such as Local Leaders, Organizations, and Justice Systems

Building partnerships is a crucial step in implementing restorative justice circles within a community. Engaging stakeholders such as local leaders, organizations, and justice systems helps create a supportive network that can facilitate the successful adoption and sustainability of restorative practices. This chapter explores the importance of building partnerships, the steps involved, and strategies for effective stakeholder engagement.

The Importance of Building Partnerships

Partnerships are vital for several reasons:

1. Resource Mobilization: Partnerships can bring together resources, expertise, and support necessary for the implementation and sustainability of restorative justice circles.

2. Community Buy-In: Engaging a diverse range of stakeholders helps to build broad-based support and buy-in from the community.

3. Collaboration and Coordination: Partnerships facilitate collaboration and coordination among different sectors, ensuring a more integrated and holistic approach.

4. Legitimacy and Credibility: Involving respected local leaders and organizations can enhance the legitimacy and credibility of the restorative justice initiative.

5. Long-Term Sustainability: Strong partnerships help to ensure the long-term sustainability of restorative justice circles by embedding them within existing community structures.

Steps in Building Partnerships

Building effective partnerships involves several key steps:

1. Identify Potential Partners:

- Mapping Stakeholders: Identify potential partners, including local leaders, community organizations, justice system representatives, schools, religious institutions, and social service agencies.

- Assessing Alignment: Assess the alignment of potential partners' values, missions, and goals with the principles of restorative justice.

2. Initiate Contact:

- Outreach: Reach out to potential partners through formal and informal channels. This could include meetings, phone calls, emails, and community events.

- Building Relationships: Focus on building relationships based on mutual trust and respect. Establishing personal connections can be crucial for gaining support.

3. Present the Case for Restorative Justice:

- Inform and Educate: Provide information and education about restorative justice principles, benefits, and potential impact on the community.

- Highlight Mutual Benefits: Emphasize how the partnership can benefit the partners as well as the broader community. Highlighting mutual interests and goals can help garner support.

4. Engage in Dialogue:

- Two-Way Communication: Engage in open and two-way communication to understand the perspectives, concerns, and interests of potential partners.

- Address Concerns: Address any concerns or misconceptions about restorative justice practices. Provide evidence and examples of successful implementations.

5. Formalize Partnerships:

- Memoranda of Understanding (MOUs): Develop MOUs or partnership agreements that outline the roles, responsibilities, and commitments of each partner.

- Collaboration Framework: Establish a framework for collaboration, including regular meetings, communication channels, and decision-making processes.

6. Foster Ongoing Engagement:

- Regular Communication: Maintain regular communication with partners to keep them informed, involved, and engaged.

- Joint Planning and Implementation: Involve partners in the planning and implementation process to ensure their active participation and contribution.

- Celebrate Successes: Acknowledge and celebrate the contributions and successes of partners to reinforce their commitment and support.

Strategies for Effective Stakeholder Engagement

Effective stakeholder engagement involves several strategies:

1. Inclusive Participation: Ensure that the partnership is inclusive and representative of the diverse voices within the community. Engage marginalized groups, youth, elders, and other underrepresented populations.

2. Transparency and Accountability: Maintain transparency in decision-making and implementation processes. Ensure that partners are accountable for their commitments and actions.

3. Flexibility and Adaptability: Be flexible and adaptable in responding to the needs and concerns of partners. Adjust plans and approaches as needed to accommodate different perspectives.

4. Capacity Building: Provide training and capacity-building opportunities for partners to enhance their understanding and skills related to restorative justice practices.

5. Mutual Respect and Trust: Foster a culture of mutual respect and trust among partners. Recognize and value the contributions and expertise of each partner.

Examples of Effective Partnerships

Example 1: School and Community Partnership

A community faced with rising incidents of bullying and conflicts in schools decided to implement restorative justice circles. The school district partnered with local community organizations, parents, and students to develop and implement the program. The partnership involved:

- Training for Teachers and Staff: Community organizations provided training for teachers and staff on restorative practices and facilitation techniques.

- Student Involvement: Students were involved in designing and leading restorative circles, promoting peer-led conflict resolution.

- Parental Engagement: Parents were engaged through workshops and informational sessions to build understanding and support for the initiative.

- Ongoing Support: The partnership established a support network for ongoing coaching and mentoring to ensure the sustainability of the program.

Example 2: Justice System and Social Services Partnership

In a city with high rates of youth crime, the justice system partnered with social service agencies to implement restorative justice circles as an alternative to traditional court proceedings. The partnership included:

- Diversion Programs: The justice system referred eligible youth offenders to restorative justice circles instead of formal prosecution.

- Case Management: Social service agencies provided case management and support services for the youth and their families, addressing underlying issues such as substance abuse, mental health, and educational needs.

- Community Involvement: Community members, including victims and local leaders, participated in the circles, contributing to the healing and reintegration process.

- Monitoring and Evaluation: The partnership established a monitoring and evaluation framework to assess the impact and effectiveness of the restorative justice circles.

Conclusion

Building partnerships is a critical step in implementing restorative justice circles within a community. Engaging stakeholders such as local leaders, organizations, and justice systems helps create a supportive network that can facilitate the successful adoption and sustainability of restorative practices. By following a structured approach to identifying, engaging, and collaborating with partners, communities can develop strong and effective partnerships that enhance the impact and reach of restorative justice circles. The involvement of diverse stakeholders ensures a holistic and integrated approach, fostering community healing, accountability, and social cohesion.

and stakeholders to ensure the training is relevant and context-specific.

Designing a Facilitator Training Program

A well-designed facilitator training program should be structured to provide comprehensive learning experiences that build both theoretical knowledge and practical skills. Here is a suggested structure:

1. Orientation Session:

- Introduction to Restorative Justice: Overview of restorative justice principles and the role of facilitators.

- Objectives and Expectations: Clear outline of the training objectives, structure, and expectations from participants.

2. Module 1: Understanding Restorative Justice Principles:

- Core Concepts: Detailed exploration of restorative justice principles such as accountability, healing, and community involvement.

- Historical Context: Overview of the history and evolution of restorative justice practices.

3. Module 2: Facilitation Skills:

- Active Listening: Techniques and exercises to develop active listening skills.

- Effective Communication: Training on clear and respectful communication, including non-verbal cues.

- Questioning Techniques: Methods for asking open-ended questions that facilitate dialogue.

4. Module 3: Managing Group Dynamics:

- Creating Safe Spaces: Strategies for fostering a safe and respectful environment.

- Balancing Participation: Techniques for ensuring equal participation and managing dominant voices.

- Conflict Resolution: Approaches to managing and resolving conflicts during the circle process.

5. Module 4: Cultural Competence:

- Diversity Awareness: Understanding and respecting cultural diversity within the community.

- Inclusive Practices: Strategies for making the circle process inclusive and culturally sensitive.

6. Module 5: Ethical Considerations:

- Confidentiality: Importance of maintaining confidentiality and handling sensitive information.

- Impartiality: Ensuring neutrality and avoiding bias in facilitation.

- Professional Boundaries: Maintaining appropriate boundaries with participants.

7. Module 6: Practical Exercises and Role-Playing:

- Simulation Exercises: Role-playing scenarios to practice facilitation skills in a controlled environment.

- Feedback and Reflection: Sessions for receiving feedback from trainers and peers, and reflecting on personal performance.

8. Module 7: Advanced Facilitation Techniques (Optional for experienced facilitators):

- Complex Case Management: Handling complex and high-conflict cases.

- Advanced Communication Skills: Deepening skills in communication and conflict resolution.

- Leadership in Circles: Developing leadership skills for guiding circles effectively.

9. Ongoing Professional Development:

- Workshops and Seminars: Regular opportunities for advanced learning and skill enhancement.

- Peer Learning Groups: Facilitator peer groups for sharing experiences and strategies.

- Continuous Evaluation: Regular performance evaluations and feedback to support continuous improvement.

Case Studies Highlighting Facilitator Training

Case Study 1: Community-Based Training Program

In a diverse urban community, a local nonprofit organization developed a comprehensive facilitator training program to support the implementation of restorative justice circles in schools and neighborhood groups. The program included:

- Partnership with Schools: Collaborated with local schools to provide training for teachers and counselors.

- Cultural Competence Workshops: Offered specialized workshops on cultural competence to address the diverse backgrounds of community members.

- Mentorship System: Established a mentorship system pairing new facilitators with experienced practitioners for guidance and support.

Case Study 2: Justice System Collaboration

In a rural area with a high rate of juvenile delinquency, the local justice system partnered with social services to develop a facilitator training program. Key features included:

- Joint Training Sessions: Combined training sessions for justice system professionals and social service providers to foster collaboration.

- Focus on Youth Engagement: Specialized training on engaging and working with youth offenders and their families.

- Ongoing Support: Provided continuous support and supervision for facilitators through regular check-ins and professional development workshops.

Conclusion

Training facilitators is a critical component of implementing restorative justice circles effectively. Well-trained facilitators are essential for guiding the circle process, managing group dynamics, and ensuring that the principles of restorative justice are upheld. A comprehensive training program that includes theoretical knowledge, practical skills, and ongoing professional development can equip facilitators to perform their roles effectively. By investing in facilitator training, communities can enhance the success and sustainability of restorative justice circles, promoting healing, accountability, and social cohesion.

Implementing Restorative Justice Circles in Communities

Creating Guidelines: Establishing Clear Procedures and Expectations for Circles

Creating clear guidelines is a crucial step in implementing restorative justice circles. Well-defined procedures and expectations ensure that the process is consistent, respectful, and effective. This chapter explores the importance of creating guidelines, the key elements to include, and strategies for developing and implementing these guidelines within a community.

The Importance of Creating Guidelines

Guidelines are essential for several reasons:

1. Consistency: Guidelines ensure that restorative justice circles are conducted in a consistent manner, providing a reliable framework for all participants.

2. Clarity: Clear procedures and expectations help participants understand their roles and responsibilities, reducing confusion and misunderstandings.

3. Respect and Safety: Guidelines establish norms for respectful behavior and communication, creating a safe environment for dialogue.

4. Effectiveness: Well-defined guidelines enhance the effectiveness of the circle process, helping to achieve meaningful resolutions and outcomes.

5. Accountability: Guidelines provide a basis for holding participants accountable to the agreed-upon process and behaviors.

Key Elements of Guidelines for Restorative Justice Circles

A comprehensive set of guidelines for restorative justice circles should include several key elements:

1. Purpose and Goals:

- Define the Purpose: Clearly articulate the purpose of the restorative justice circle, whether it is to address a specific conflict, support a victim, or reintegrate an offender.

- Set Goals: Establish specific goals for the circle, such as fostering understanding, promoting healing, or developing a reparation plan.

2. Participation and Roles:

- Identify Participants: Specify who will participate in the circle, including victims, offenders, community members, and facilitators.

- Define Roles: Clearly define the roles and responsibilities of each participant, including the facilitator's role in guiding the process.

3. Preparation:

- Pre-Circle Meetings: Outline the procedures for pre-circle meetings with participants to explain the process, address concerns, and prepare them for the circle.

- Information Sharing: Establish guidelines for sharing information and setting expectations before the circle begins.

4. Circle Structure and Process:

- Opening and Closing: Define the opening and closing rituals or statements to set the tone and provide closure to the circle.

- Talking Piece: Specify the use of a talking piece to ensure that everyone has an equal opportunity to speak and be heard.

- Turn-Taking: Establish a method for turn-taking to ensure that all participants have a chance to contribute.

5. Ground Rules for Behavior:

- Respectful Communication: Set ground rules for respectful communication, including active listening, speaking from personal experience, and avoiding blame or judgment.

- Confidentiality: Define the confidentiality expectations, ensuring that what is shared in the circle remains private.

- Non-Violence: Emphasize the importance of non-violence and maintaining a safe environment for all participants.

6. Decision-Making and Agreements:

- Consensus Building: Outline the process for building consensus and reaching agreements on how to address the harm and move forward.

- Documentation: Establish guidelines for documenting agreements and ensuring that all parties understand and commit to the agreed-upon actions.

7. Follow-Up and Support:

- Post-Circle Follow-Up: Specify procedures for post-circle follow-up meetings to review progress, address any ongoing issues, and provide additional support.

- Support Resources: Provide information about available support resources, such as counseling, mediation, or community services.

Strategies for Developing and Implementing Guidelines

Developing and implementing guidelines involves several steps:

1. Collaborative Development:

- Involve Stakeholders: Engage key stakeholders, including community members, facilitators, and justice system representatives, in the development of guidelines to ensure that they are relevant and context-specific.

- Community Input: Seek input from the broader community through surveys, focus groups, or public meetings to gather diverse perspectives and build consensus.

2. Drafting Guidelines:

- Clear and Accessible Language: Use clear and accessible language to draft the guidelines, ensuring that they are easy to understand for all participants.

- Comprehensive and Specific: Ensure that the guidelines are comprehensive and specific, covering all key elements and potential scenarios.

3. Review and Approval:

- Feedback and Revision: Circulate the draft guidelines for feedback and make revisions based on input from stakeholders.

- Formal Approval: Seek formal approval from relevant authorities or governing bodies to validate the guidelines and provide official support.

4. Training and Orientation:

- Facilitator Training: Provide training for facilitators on the guidelines, ensuring that they are well-versed in the procedures and expectations.

- Participant Orientation: Conduct orientation sessions for participants to explain the guidelines and answer any questions they may have.

5. Implementation and Monitoring:

- Consistent Application: Ensure that the guidelines are consistently applied in all restorative justice circles.

\- Monitoring and Evaluation: Implement mechanisms for monitoring and evaluating the effectiveness of the guidelines, including gathering feedback from participants.

6. Ongoing Review and Improvement:

\- Regular Review: Regularly review the guidelines to ensure that they remain relevant and effective.

\- Continuous Improvement: Make adjustments and improvements to the guidelines based on feedback and changing community needs.

Case Studies Highlighting Guideline Development

Case Study 1: School-Based Restorative Justice Circles

A high school implemented restorative justice circles to address conflicts and promote a positive school culture. The process included:

\- Collaborative Development: The school administration, teachers, students, and parents collaborated to develop the guidelines.

\- Clear Structure: The guidelines included clear procedures for opening and closing circles, using a talking piece, and managing turn-taking.

\- Respectful Communication: Ground rules emphasized respectful communication, confidentiality, and non-violence.

- Training and Orientation: The school provided training for facilitators and orientation sessions for students and staff to ensure understanding and adherence to the guidelines.

Case Study 2: Community-Based Restorative Justice Circles

A community organization developed restorative justice circles to address neighborhood disputes and minor offenses. The process involved:

- Community Input: The organization sought input from community members through public meetings and surveys to develop the guidelines.

- Inclusive Participation: The guidelines specified the roles of participants, including victims, offenders, and community representatives.

- Consensus Building: Procedures for consensus building and reaching agreements were clearly defined.

- Ongoing Support: Follow-up procedures and support resources were included to ensure the sustainability of the agreements.

Conclusion

Creating clear guidelines is essential for the successful implementation of restorative justice circles. Well-defined procedures and expectations ensure consistency, clarity, respect, and effectiveness, providing a reliable framework for participants and facilitators. By developing comprehensive guidelines through a collaborative process and ensuring their consistent application, communities can enhance the impact and sustainability of restorative justice circles, promoting healing, accountability, and social cohesion.

CHAPTER 05

THE ROLE OF FACILITATORS IN RESTORATIVE JUSTICE CIRCLES

Facilitators play a crucial role in restorative justice circles, guiding the process and ensuring a safe and respectful environment. This chapter discusses the qualities and skills of effective facilitators, their responsibilities, and the training required to prepare them for this role.

Qualities of Effective Facilitators

Effective facilitators possess a combination of personal qualities that enable them to guide restorative justice circles successfully. These qualities include:

1. Empathy: Facilitators must be able to understand and share the feelings of participants, creating an environment where individuals feel heard and validated.

2. Impartiality: Maintaining neutrality and avoiding bias is essential for facilitators to ensure that all voices are equally valued.

3. Patience: Facilitators need patience to allow the process to unfold naturally and to manage any challenges that arise without rushing or forcing resolutions.

4. Integrity: Honesty and ethical behavior are critical for building trust and credibility with participants.

5. Open-mindedness: Being open to diverse perspectives and experiences helps facilitators manage the circle process effectively and inclusively.

6. Resilience: Facilitators must be resilient to handle emotionally charged situations and maintain their own well-being.

Skills of Effective Facilitators

In addition to personal qualities, effective facilitators must have specific skills to guide restorative justice circles:

1. Active Listening: The ability to listen attentively and respond appropriately to participants, ensuring they feel heard and understood.

2. Effective Communication: Clear and respectful communication is essential for guiding discussions and managing group dynamics.

3. Conflict Resolution: Facilitators must be skilled in resolving conflicts and de-escalating tense situations.

4. Questioning Techniques: Using open-ended questions to encourage reflection and dialogue among participants.

5. Group Facilitation: Managing group dynamics, ensuring equal participation, and creating a safe and respectful environment.

6. Cultural Competence: Understanding and respecting cultural differences, and incorporating inclusive practices into the circle process.

7. Ethical Decision-Making: Navigating ethical dilemmas and maintaining professional boundaries.

Responsibilities of Facilitators

Facilitators have several key responsibilities in restorative justice circles:

1. Preparation:

- Pre-Circle Meetings: Conducting pre-circle meetings with participants to explain the process, address concerns, and prepare them for the circle.

- Logistical Arrangements: Ensuring that all logistical arrangements, such as venue, seating, and materials, are in place for the circle.

2. Guiding the Circle Process:

- Setting the Tone: Opening the circle with a welcoming statement or ritual to set a positive and respectful tone.

- Managing the Process: Guiding the discussion, managing turn-taking, and using a talking piece to ensure that everyone has an opportunity to speak.

- Maintaining Safety: Ensuring that the circle remains a safe space for all participants, addressing any disruptive behavior or conflicts that arise.

3. Facilitating Dialogue:

- Encouraging Participation: Encouraging all participants to share their perspectives and actively engaging quieter members.

- Asking Questions: Using open-ended questions to prompt reflection and deeper dialogue.

- Building Consensus: Helping participants build consensus and reach agreements on how to address the harm and move forward.

4. Post-Circle Follow-Up:

- Documenting Agreements: Ensuring that agreements reached during the circle are documented and understood by all participants.

- Providing Support: Offering support and resources to participants after the circle, including follow-up meetings if needed.

Training for Facilitators

Comprehensive training is essential to prepare facilitators for their role in restorative justice circles. Key components of facilitator training include:

1. Understanding Restorative Justice Principles:

- Core Concepts: Training should cover the core principles of restorative justice, including healing, accountability, and community involvement.

- Historical Context: Providing an overview of the history and evolution of restorative justice to contextualize its practices.

2. Developing Facilitation Skills:

- Active Listening: Techniques and exercises to develop active listening skills.

- Effective Communication: Training on clear and respectful communication, including non-verbal cues.

- Questioning Techniques: Methods for asking open-ended questions that facilitate dialogue.

3. Managing Group Dynamics:

- Creating Safe Spaces: Strategies for fostering a safe and respectful environment.

- Balancing Participation: Techniques for ensuring equal participation and managing dominant voices.

- Conflict Resolution: Approaches to managing and resolving conflicts during the circle process.

4. Cultural Competence:

- Understanding Diversity: Training to recognize and respect cultural diversity within the community.

- Inclusive Practices: Strategies for making the circle process inclusive and culturally sensitive.

5. Ethical Considerations:

- Confidentiality: Importance of maintaining confidentiality and handling sensitive information.

- Impartiality: Ensuring neutrality and avoiding bias in facilitation.

- Professional Boundaries: Maintaining appropriate boundaries with participants.

6. Practical Exercises and Role-Playing:

- Simulation Exercises: Role-playing scenarios to practice facilitation skills in a controlled environment.

- Feedback and Reflection: Sessions for receiving feedback from trainers and peers, and reflecting on personal performance.

7. Ongoing Professional Development:

- Advanced Training: Opportunities for advanced training and workshops to deepen skills and knowledge.

- Peer Learning: Facilitator peer groups for sharing experiences and strategies.

- Continuous Evaluation: Regular performance evaluations and feedback to support continuous improvement.

Case Studies Highlighting Facilitator Roles

Case Study 1: School-Based Restorative Justice Circles

In a high school, trained facilitators played a key role in implementing restorative justice circles to address bullying and conflicts. Their responsibilities included:

- Pre-Circle Meetings: Conducting meetings with students and parents to prepare them for the circle process.

- Guiding Discussions: Facilitators used active listening and questioning techniques to guide discussions and ensure respectful communication.

- Building Consensus: Helping students reach agreements on how to repair harm and improve relationships.

Case Study 2: Community-Based Restorative Justice Circles

In a neighborhood affected by vandalism, trained facilitators guided restorative justice circles involving offenders, victims, and community members. Their responsibilities included:

- Creating Safe Spaces: Establishing ground rules for respectful behavior and ensuring a safe environment.

- Encouraging Participation: Actively engaging all participants and encouraging quieter members to share their perspectives.

- Documenting Agreements: Ensuring that agreements reached during the circle were documented and understood by all parties.

Conclusion

Facilitators play a crucial role in restorative justice circles, guiding the process and ensuring a safe and respectful environment. Effective facilitators possess a combination of personal qualities and skills that enable them to manage group dynamics, facilitate dialogue, and promote healing and accountability. Comprehensive training is essential to prepare facilitators for their role, covering key principles, facilitation skills, cultural competence, and ethical considerations. By investing in the training and development of facilitators, communities can enhance the effectiveness and sustainability of restorative justice circles, promoting positive outcomes for all participants.

CHAPTER 06

THE CIRCLE PROCESS: STEPS AND PROCEDURES

Preparation: Meeting with Participants Individually to Explain the Process and Address Concerns

Preparation is a critical first step in the restorative justice circle process. Meeting with participants individually before the circle convenes helps ensure that everyone understands the process, addresses any concerns they may have, and prepares them for meaningful participation. This chapter explores the importance of preparation, the steps involved in meeting with participants, and strategies for addressing common concerns.

The Importance of Preparation

Effective preparation is essential for several reasons:

1. Understanding the Process: Individual meetings provide an opportunity to explain the restorative justice circle process in detail, ensuring that all participants understand what to expect.

2. Building Trust: These meetings help build trust between facilitators and participants, establishing a foundation for open and honest dialogue during the circle.

3. Addressing Concerns: Participants may have concerns or fears about the process. Addressing these concerns beforehand helps alleviate anxiety and increase their comfort level.

4. Ensuring Readiness: Preparation helps assess the readiness of participants to engage in the circle, ensuring that they are emotionally and mentally prepared.

5. Clarifying Roles: It provides a chance to clarify the roles and responsibilities of each participant, ensuring that everyone understands their part in the process.

Steps in the Preparation Process

The preparation process involves several key steps:

1. Scheduling Individual Meetings:

- Initial Contact: Reach out to participants to schedule individual meetings. Ensure that the timing and location are convenient for them.

- Flexible Scheduling: Offer flexibility in scheduling to accommodate participants' availability and preferences.

2. Explaining the Circle Process:

- Overview of Restorative Justice: Provide an overview of restorative justice principles and how the circle process aligns with these principles.

- Detailed Explanation: Explain the specific steps and procedures of the circle process, including the use of a talking piece, turn-taking, and consensus-building.

3. Addressing Concerns and Questions:

- Open Dialogue: Encourage participants to express any concerns or questions they may have about the process.

- Providing Reassurance: Offer reassurance and support, addressing concerns empathetically and providing clear, concise answers.

4. Assessing Readiness:

- Emotional Readiness: Assess participants' emotional readiness to engage in the circle, considering factors such as recent trauma or unresolved anger.

- Willingness to Participate: Ensure that participants are willing to participate voluntarily and understand the importance of their role in the process.

5. Clarifying Roles and Responsibilities:

- Participant Roles: Clarify the roles of each participant, including victims, offenders, community members, and facilitators.

- Facilitator's Role: Explain the facilitator's role in guiding the process and ensuring a respectful and safe environment.

6. Setting Expectations:

- Ground Rules: Discuss the ground rules for the circle, such as respectful communication, confidentiality, and non-violence.

- Desired Outcomes: Outline the desired outcomes of the circle, including healing, accountability, and reparation.

7. Providing Information and Resources:

- Educational Materials: Provide educational materials, such as brochures or handouts, that explain the circle process and restorative justice principles.

- Support Resources: Offer information about support resources, such as counseling services, that participants can access if needed.

Strategies for Effective Preparation

Effective preparation involves several strategies to ensure that participants are well-informed and comfortable with the process:

1. Active Listening:

- Empathetic Listening: Practice active and empathetic listening during individual meetings, showing genuine interest in participants' concerns and perspectives.

- Reflective Responses: Use reflective responses to validate participants' feelings and ensure that they feel heard and understood.

2. Clear and Concise Communication:

- Simplify Explanations: Use clear and simple language to explain the circle process, avoiding jargon or technical terms.

- Visual Aids: Utilize visual aids, such as diagrams or flowcharts, to help illustrate the steps and procedures of the circle process.

3. Building Rapport:

- Personal Connection: Establish a personal connection with participants by showing empathy and understanding.

- Trust-Building: Engage in trust-building activities, such as sharing personal experiences or stories that highlight the benefits of restorative justice.

4. Flexibility and Adaptability:

- Adapt to Needs: Be flexible and adaptable in responding to participants' needs and preferences. Adjust the approach as necessary to accommodate different personalities and situations.

- Individualized Support: Provide individualized support, recognizing that each participant may have unique concerns and requirements.

5. Creating a Safe Environment:

- Confidentiality Assurance: Assure participants that their discussions during preparation meetings are confidential and will not be shared without their consent.

- Non-Judgmental Approach: Maintain a non-judgmental approach, creating a safe space for participants to express their thoughts and feelings openly.

Addressing Common Concerns

Participants may have various concerns about the restorative justice circle process. Common concerns and strategies for addressing them include:

1. Fear of Confrontation:

- Reassure Safety: Reassure participants that the process is designed to be safe and respectful, with facilitators managing the dialogue to prevent confrontation.

- Explain Structure: Explain the structured nature of the circle, including the use of a talking piece and turn-taking, to ensure that everyone has a chance to speak without interruption.

2. Confidentiality Worries:

- Clarify Confidentiality: Clearly explain the confidentiality guidelines and the importance of maintaining privacy within the circle.

- Provide Examples: Share examples of how confidentiality is upheld in similar processes to build trust.

3. Doubt about Effectiveness:

- Share Success Stories: Share success stories and case studies that demonstrate the effectiveness of restorative justice circles in similar situations.

- Highlight Benefits: Highlight the potential benefits of the process, including healing, accountability, and community restoration.

4. Emotional Readiness:

- Assess and Support: Assess participants' emotional readiness and provide support resources, such as counseling, if needed.

- Offer Alternatives: If participants are not ready, discuss alternative restorative practices or timelines that may be more suitable.

5. Uncertainty about Participation:

- Voluntary Nature: Emphasize the voluntary nature of participation and the importance of their choice in engaging with the process.

- Role Clarification: Clarify the specific role they will play and how their participation contributes to the overall goals of the circle.

Case Study: Effective Preparation in Practice

Case Study: Community Restorative Justice Circle Preparation

In a community dealing with a series of neighborhood conflicts, facilitators implemented a restorative justice circle process. The preparation phase included:

- Individual Meetings: Facilitators scheduled individual meetings with all participants, including victims, offenders, and community members.

- Explaining the Process: During these meetings, facilitators provided a detailed explanation of the circle process, using visual aids and simple language.

- Addressing Concerns: Participants were encouraged to voice their concerns, which were addressed empathetically and thoroughly by the facilitators.

- Building Trust: Facilitators focused on building trust and rapport, ensuring that participants felt comfortable and understood the importance of their involvement.

- Clarifying Roles: The roles and responsibilities of each participant were clarified, and ground rules for the circle were discussed and agreed upon.

As a result of effective preparation, the restorative justice circle was conducted smoothly, with participants feeling supported and ready to engage in the process. The circle led to meaningful resolutions and strengthened community bonds.

Conclusion

Preparation is a critical step in the restorative justice circle process, ensuring that participants are informed, comfortable, and ready to engage. By conducting individual meetings, explaining the process, addressing concerns, and building trust, facilitators can create a strong foundation for a successful circle. Effective preparation involves clear communication, active listening, and a supportive approach tailored to the needs of each participant. By investing time and effort in the preparation phase, communities can enhance the effectiveness and impact of restorative justice circles, promoting healing, accountability, and social cohesion.

The Circle Process: Steps and Procedures

Opening: Setting the Tone with a Welcoming Statement or Ritual

The opening of a restorative justice circle is a crucial step that sets the tone for the entire process. A well-structured opening helps establish a safe and respectful environment, encourages trust, and prepares participants for meaningful dialogue. This chapter explores the importance of the opening, various elements that can be included, and strategies for creating an effective and welcoming introduction to the circle.

The Importance of the Opening

The opening of a restorative justice circle serves several important purposes:

1. Establishing a Safe Environment: A welcoming statement or ritual helps create a sense of safety and respect, reassuring participants that the circle is a supportive space.

2. Setting the Tone: The opening sets the tone for the circle, emphasizing the values of respect, empathy, and collaboration.

3. Building Trust: A thoughtful opening helps build trust among participants, encouraging openness and honesty.

4. Focusing Attention: The opening brings participants' attention to the present moment, helping them to be fully engaged in the process.

5. Reinforcing Ground Rules: It provides an opportunity to remind participants of the ground rules and expectations for behavior during the circle.

Elements of an Effective Opening

An effective opening for a restorative justice circle can include several key elements:

1. Welcoming Statement:

- Introduction: A brief introduction by the facilitator to welcome participants and express gratitude for their presence.

- Purpose of the Circle: A clear explanation of the purpose and goals of the circle.

2. Ritual or Ceremony:

- Cultural Practices: Incorporating cultural or traditional practices relevant to the participants, such as a prayer, song, or moment of silence.

- Symbolic Actions: Simple, symbolic actions that signify the start of the circle, such as lighting a candle or passing a symbolic object.

3. Ground Rules and Expectations:

- Review Ground Rules: A reminder of the ground rules for respectful communication, confidentiality, and non-violence.

- Setting Expectations: Clear expectations for participation, including the use of a talking piece and turn-taking.

4. Icebreakers and Introductions:

- Participant Introductions: Allowing participants to introduce themselves and share something about their role or connection to the circle.

- Icebreaker Activities: Simple icebreaker activities to help participants feel more comfortable and connected.

5. Mindfulness and Centering:

- Mindfulness Exercises: Brief mindfulness or centering exercises to help participants focus and become present.

- Breathing Techniques: Guided breathing exercises to promote relaxation and readiness for dialogue.

Strategies for Creating an Effective Opening

Creating an effective opening involves thoughtful planning and consideration of the participants' needs and context. Here are some strategies for crafting a welcoming and impactful opening:

1. Tailor to the Audience:

- Cultural Sensitivity: Consider the cultural backgrounds and traditions of the participants when designing the opening.

- Relevance: Ensure that the opening is relevant to the specific issues and goals of the circle.

2. Be Inclusive:

- Invite Participation: Encourage participants to contribute to the opening, such as sharing a quote or leading a ritual.

- Respect Diversity: Acknowledge and respect the diverse perspectives and experiences of participants.

3. Create a Sense of Ritual:

- Consistency: Use consistent opening rituals or statements in each circle to create a sense of familiarity and comfort.

- Symbolism: Incorporate symbolic elements that resonate with participants and enhance the sense of purpose.

4. Use Clear and Positive Language:

- Clarity: Use clear and straightforward language to explain the purpose and process of the circle.

- Positivity: Emphasize positive values such as respect, empathy, and collaboration.

5. Foster Connection:

- Personal Stories: Share a brief personal story or anecdote that highlights the importance of restorative justice.

- Encourage Sharing: Create opportunities for participants to share their thoughts and feelings during the opening.

Examples of Effective Openings

Example 1: School-Based Restorative Justice Circle

In a high school setting, the facilitator opens a restorative justice circle with the following steps:

1. Welcoming Statement: "Welcome, everyone. Thank you for being here today. This circle is a space for us to come together, listen to each other, and find ways to address the harm that has occurred."

2. Purpose of the Circle: "Our goal today is to understand the impact of the recent conflict, support those affected, and work towards healing and resolution."

3. Ground Rules: "Let's remember our ground rules: speak from the heart, listen with respect, maintain confidentiality, and use the talking piece when it's your turn to speak."

4. Icebreaker Activity: Participants are asked to share their names and one word that describes how they are feeling at that moment.

5. Mindfulness Exercise: A brief guided breathing exercise to help everyone focus and center themselves.

Example 2: Community Restorative Justice Circle

In a community setting, the facilitator opens the circle with these elements:

1. Welcoming Statement: "Good evening, everyone. I'm grateful to see you all here. This circle is a safe space where

we can come together to address the issues affecting our community."

2. Purpose of the Circle: "Tonight, we will discuss the recent incidents of vandalism and explore how we can work together to repair the harm and strengthen our community bonds."

3. Cultural Ritual: A community elder leads a traditional blessing or prayer to honor the cultural heritage of the participants.

4. Ground Rules: "Please remember to respect each other's voices, keep our discussions confidential, and speak one at a time using the talking piece."

5. Participant Introductions: Each participant introduces themselves and shares their connection to the community.

6. Centering Exercise: A moment of silence to reflect on the shared goal of healing and reconciliation.

Conclusion

The opening of a restorative justice circle is a critical step that sets the tone for the entire process. By incorporating a welcoming statement or ritual, reviewing ground rules, and fostering connection, facilitators can create a safe and respectful environment for meaningful dialogue. An effective opening helps build trust, focus attention, and prepare participants for the collaborative journey ahead. Thoughtful planning and consideration of the participants' needs and context are essential for crafting an impactful and welcoming introduction to the circle.

Sharing: Participants Take Turns Speaking, Following Established Guidelines

The sharing phase of a restorative justice circle is where participants take turns speaking and sharing their experiences, thoughts, and feelings about the harm that has occurred. This phase is crucial for fostering understanding, empathy, and healing. Effective sharing follows established guidelines to ensure that every participant has an equal opportunity to speak and be heard. This chapter explores the importance of sharing, the guidelines for effective sharing, and strategies for facilitating this phase of the circle process.

The Importance of Sharing

Sharing is a central component of the restorative justice circle process for several reasons:

1. Fostering Understanding: Sharing personal experiences and perspectives helps participants understand the impact of the harm on everyone involved.

2. Building Empathy: Listening to others' stories fosters empathy, encouraging participants to connect with each other's emotions and experiences.

3. Promoting Healing: Sharing feelings and experiences can be cathartic, helping participants process their emotions and begin healing.

4. Ensuring Inclusivity: Taking turns speaking ensures that all voices are heard, promoting a sense of inclusivity and respect.

5. Facilitating Accountability: Offenders have the opportunity to hear firsthand the impact of their actions, which can promote accountability and remorse.

Guidelines for Effective Sharing

Effective sharing in a restorative justice circle follows several key guidelines:

1. Use of a Talking Piece:

- Symbol of Respect: A talking piece is passed around the circle, symbolizing respect and ensuring that only the person holding it speaks.

- Equal Opportunity: This practice ensures that everyone has an equal opportunity to speak without interruption.

2. Active Listening:

- Focus on the Speaker: Participants should listen actively, giving their full attention to the speaker.

- Non-Verbal Cues: Show engagement through non-verbal cues such as nodding and maintaining eye contact.

3. Speaking from the Heart:

- Personal Experiences: Encourage participants to share their personal experiences and feelings rather than making generalized statements or accusations.

- Honesty and Vulnerability: Promote honesty and vulnerability, creating a space where participants feel safe to express their true emotions.

4. Respectful Communication:

- No Interruptions: Ensure that participants do not interrupt each other, allowing everyone to speak fully.

- Non-Judgmental: Foster a non-judgmental atmosphere where participants feel free to share without fear of criticism or blame.

5. Confidentiality:

- Privacy of Sharing: Remind participants of the importance of maintaining confidentiality about what is shared in the circle.

- Safe Space: Reinforce the idea that the circle is a safe space for open and honest communication.

Strategies for Facilitating Effective Sharing

Facilitators play a crucial role in guiding the sharing phase of the circle process. Here are some strategies for facilitating effective sharing:

1. Setting the Tone:

- Opening Remarks: Begin the sharing phase with opening remarks that emphasize the importance of respectful communication and active listening.

- Modeling Behavior: Model the desired behavior by demonstrating active listening and respectful communication.

2. Using the Talking Piece:

- Introduction of the Talking Piece: Introduce the talking piece and explain its significance in promoting respectful and equal participation.

- Ensuring Turn-Taking: Ensure that the talking piece is passed around the circle in an orderly manner, allowing everyone a chance to speak.

3. Encouraging Participation:

- Inviting Quiet Participants: Gently encourage quieter participants to share, ensuring that all voices are heard.

- Validating Contributions: Validate each participant's contribution, acknowledging their experiences and feelings.

4. Managing Time:

- Balanced Speaking Time: Monitor the time each participant speaks to ensure that everyone has an equal opportunity to share.

- Pacing the Discussion: Pace the discussion to allow for thoughtful reflection and meaningful dialogue.

5. Addressing Emotional Intensity:

- Supporting Emotional Expression: Support participants in expressing their emotions, providing reassurance and empathy.

- Managing Distress: Be prepared to manage emotional distress, offering breaks or additional support if needed.

6. Facilitating Reflection:

- Reflective Questions: Use reflective questions to deepen the discussion and encourage participants to think more deeply about their experiences.

- Encouraging Connection: Encourage participants to reflect on how their experiences connect to those of others in the circle.

Examples of Effective Sharing

Example 1: School-Based Restorative Justice Circle

In a high school setting, a restorative justice circle is convened to address a conflict between students. The facilitator uses the following approach for effective sharing:

1. Introduction of the Talking Piece: The facilitator introduces a symbolic object, such as a decorated stick, as the talking piece.

2. Setting Ground Rules: Ground rules are reviewed, emphasizing respectful communication, no interruptions, and confidentiality.

3. Opening Round: Each student is invited to share their name and one feeling they are experiencing about the conflict.

4. Encouraging Vulnerability: The facilitator gently encourages students to share their personal experiences and feelings related to the conflict.

5. Active Listening: Students are reminded to listen actively and respectfully to each speaker, using non-verbal cues to show engagement.

Example 2: Community Restorative Justice Circle

In a community affected by a series of burglaries, a restorative justice circle is organized to address the harm and promote healing. The facilitator ensures effective sharing with the following steps:

1. Opening Remarks: The facilitator opens with remarks that emphasize the importance of listening and sharing from the heart.

2. Introduction of the Talking Piece: A small stone is introduced as the talking piece, symbolizing the weight of each person's story.

3. Structured Sharing: Participants take turns sharing their experiences, using the talking piece to manage turn-taking.

4. Validating Feelings: The facilitator validates each participant's feelings and experiences, acknowledging the impact of the harm on their lives.

5. Encouraging Empathy: Reflective questions are used to encourage participants to consider how others may be feeling and to build empathy.

Conclusion

The sharing phase of a restorative justice circle is essential for fostering understanding, empathy, and healing among participants. By following established guidelines, such as using a talking piece, practicing active listening, and promoting respectful communication, facilitators can create a safe and inclusive environment for meaningful dialogue. Effective sharing allows participants to express their feelings and experiences openly, building connections and promoting accountability. Thoughtful facilitation and adherence to guidelines ensure that the sharing phase contributes to the overall goals of the restorative justice circle, promoting healing and resolution.

Discussion: Engaging in Dialogue to Explore the Harm, Its Impact, and Possible Resolutions

The discussion phase of a restorative justice circle is where participants engage in dialogue to explore the harm that has occurred, understand its impact on all parties, and collaboratively seek possible resolutions. This phase is crucial for fostering deeper understanding, and empathy, and developing actionable steps toward healing and reconciliation. This chapter delves into the importance of the discussion phase, the strategies for facilitating effective dialogue, and the steps involved in exploring harm and resolutions.

The Importance of Discussion

The discussion phase is a critical component of the restorative justice circle for several reasons:

1. Deepening Understanding: Engaging in dialogue allows participants to gain a deeper understanding of the harm, its causes, and its effects on everyone involved.

2. Fostering Empathy: Through open and honest conversation, participants can develop empathy for each other, recognizing shared humanity and the complexities of the situation.

3. Collaborative Problem-Solving: The discussion phase provides a platform for collaborative problem-solving, where participants work together to identify solutions and make amends.

4. Building Trust: Open dialogue builds trust among participants, creating a foundation for genuine reconciliation and healing.

5. Empowering Participants: Allowing everyone to voice their thoughts and contribute to the resolution process empowers participants and promotes a sense of ownership in the outcomes.

Strategies for Facilitating Effective Discussion

Facilitators play a vital role in guiding the discussion phase, ensuring that it is productive, respectful, and focused. Here are some strategies for facilitating effective discussions:

1. Setting the Stage:

- Establish Ground Rules: Reinforce the ground rules established during the opening phase, emphasizing respect, active listening, and confidentiality.

- Create a Safe Environment: Ensure that the environment is safe and supportive, where participants feel comfortable expressing their thoughts and emotions.

2. Using Open-Ended Questions:

- Encourage Reflection: Ask open-ended questions that encourage participants to reflect on their experiences and the impact of the harm.

- Promote Dialogue: Use questions that promote dialogue and exploration, rather than yes/no questions or those that can be answered briefly.

3. Active Listening and Validation:

- Listen Actively: Demonstrate active listening by paying full attention, nodding, and providing verbal affirmations.

- Validate Feelings: Acknowledge and validate participants' feelings and experiences, showing empathy and understanding.

4. Managing Group Dynamics:

- Ensure Equal Participation: Encourage all participants to contribute to the discussion, gently prompting quieter members to share their perspectives.

- Address Conflicts: Be prepared to address conflicts or tensions that arise, using conflict resolution techniques to keep the discussion constructive.

5. Keeping Focus:

- Stay on Topic: Keep the discussion focused on exploring the harm, its impact, and potential resolutions. Gently steer conversations back on track if they stray.

- Summarize Key Points: Periodically summarize key points and insights to ensure clarity and keep the discussion moving forward.

Steps in the Discussion Phase

The discussion phase involves several key steps to explore the harm, its impact, and possible resolutions:

1. Exploring the Harm:

- Identify the Harm: Begin by clearly identifying the harm that has occurred. Encourage participants to describe what happened and how it has affected them.

- Share Perspectives: Allow each participant to share their perspective on the harm, including their thoughts, feelings, and experiences.

2. Understanding the Impact:

- Discuss the Impact: Facilitate a discussion on the impact of the harm on individuals and the community. Ask questions such as, "How has this affected you?" and "What changes have you noticed in your life since the incident?"

- Acknowledge Emotions: Recognize and validate the emotions expressed by participants, creating a space for honest emotional expression.

3. Identifying Needs:

- Express Needs: Encourage participants to express their needs and what they feel is necessary for healing and moving forward. This could include apologies, restitution, or changes in behavior.

- Understand Each Other's Needs: Foster an understanding of each participant's needs, helping everyone see the situation from multiple perspectives.

4. Brainstorming Resolutions:

- Generate Ideas: Facilitate a brainstorming session to generate ideas for how the harm can be repaired and future harm prevented. Encourage creative and practical solutions.

- Collaborate on Solutions: Work together to evaluate the feasibility and appropriateness of different solutions. Aim for consensus on the best way forward.

5. Developing an Action Plan:

- Create an Action Plan: Develop a concrete action plan that outlines specific steps to be taken to repair the harm and address participants' needs.

- Assign Responsibilities: Clearly assign responsibilities for each action item, ensuring that everyone knows their role in the resolution process.

6. Commitment to Follow-Up:

- Plan Follow-Up: Schedule follow-up meetings or check-ins to review progress and address any ongoing issues.

- Maintain Accountability: Establish mechanisms for accountability to ensure that commitments are honored and actions are taken.

Examples of Effective Discussion

Example 1: School-Based Restorative Justice Circle

In a high school, a restorative justice circle addresses a bullying incident. The facilitator guides the discussion with the following approach:

1. Exploring the Harm: The facilitator asks the bullied student to share their experience, followed by the bully sharing their perspective.

2. Understanding the Impact: Participants discuss the impact of the bullying on the victim, the bully, and the school environment.

3. Identifying Needs: The victim expresses a need for a sincere apology and assurance that the bullying will not continue. The bully expresses a need for support in changing their behavior.

4. Brainstorming Resolutions: The group brainstorms solutions, including a formal apology, a peer support group for the bully, and educational workshops on bullying prevention.

5. Developing an Action Plan: An action plan is created, outlining the steps for the apology, support group meetings, and workshops. Responsibilities are assigned to the facilitator, school counselor, and students.

Example 2: Community Restorative Justice Circle

In a neighborhood affected by vandalism, a restorative justice circle is held to address the harm. The facilitator guides the discussion with these steps:

1. Exploring the Harm: Community members affected by vandalism share their experiences and the impact on their sense of safety and property.

2. Understanding the Impact: The discussion highlights the broader impact on community trust and cohesion.

3. Identifying Needs: Victims express the need for repair of damaged property and community reassurance. Offenders express the need for forgiveness and a chance to make amends.

4. Brainstorming Resolutions: The group brainstorms ideas such as a community cleanup day, restitution for damages, and community-building activities.

5. Developing an Action Plan: A detailed action plan is developed, including dates for the cleanup day, a schedule for restitution payments, and a plan for community events. Responsibilities are assigned to offenders, community leaders, and volunteers.

Conclusion

The discussion phase of a restorative justice circle is vital for exploring the harm, understanding its impact, and developing resolutions. By fostering open dialogue, empathy, and collaborative problem-solving, this phase helps participants move toward healing and reconciliation. Effective facilitation, adherence to guidelines, and strategic planning are essential for a productive discussion phase. By engaging in meaningful dialogue, participants can achieve deeper understanding, build trust, and work together to repair the harm and prevent future incidents.

Agreement: Reaching a Consensus on How to Repair the Harm and Prevent Future Occurrences

The agreement phase of a restorative justice circle is where participants reach a consensus on how to repair the harm caused by the incident and establish measures to prevent future occurrences. This phase is crucial for ensuring that the restorative justice process leads to tangible outcomes and promotes accountability and healing. This chapter explores the importance of the agreement phase, the steps involved in reaching a consensus, and strategies for facilitating this process effectively.

The Importance of the Agreement Phase

The agreement phase is essential for several reasons:

1. Ensuring Accountability: Reaching an agreement ensures that offenders take responsibility for their actions and commit to making amends.

2. Promoting Healing: A clear agreement helps victims feel heard and validated, contributing to their healing process.

3. Preventing Future Harm: By addressing the root causes of the harm and establishing preventative measures, the agreement helps reduce the likelihood of future incidents.

4. Building Trust: Collaborative decision-making fosters trust among participants, reinforcing the community's commitment to mutual respect and support.

5. Creating a Clear Path Forward: A well-defined agreement provides a clear path forward, outlining specific actions and responsibilities for repairing the harm.

Steps in Reaching an Agreement

Reaching an agreement involves several key steps:

1. Summarizing Key Points:

- Reviewing Discussion Highlights: The facilitator summarizes the key points from the discussion phase, including the identified harms, impacts, and needs.

- Ensuring Clarity: Ensure that all participants understand and agree on the key issues discussed.

2. Identifying Possible Actions:

- Brainstorming Solutions: Facilitate a brainstorming session to generate potential actions to repair the harm and address participants' needs.

- Evaluating Options: Evaluate the feasibility, appropriateness, and potential impact of each suggested action.

3. Building Consensus:

- Encouraging Participation: Ensure that all participants have an opportunity to contribute to the decision-making process.

- Seeking Agreement: Work towards a consensus on the most appropriate actions, aiming for solutions that all participants can support.

4. Drafting the Agreement:

- Detailing Actions: Clearly outline the specific actions that will be taken to repair the harm and prevent future occurrences.

- Assigning Responsibilities: Assign responsibilities for each action, ensuring that everyone understands their role in implementing the agreement.

5. Documenting the Agreement:

- Written Record: Create a written record of the agreement, detailing the actions, responsibilities, and timelines.

- Review and Approval: Review the written agreement with all participants to ensure accuracy and obtain their approval.

6. Establishing Follow-Up:

- Setting Check-In Dates: Schedule follow-up meetings to review progress and address any ongoing issues.

- Monitoring Implementation: Establish mechanisms for monitoring the implementation of the agreement and ensuring accountability.

Strategies for Facilitating the Agreement Phase

Facilitators play a crucial role in guiding participants through the agreement phase. Here are some strategies for facilitating this process effectively:

1. Fostering Collaborative Decision-Making:

- Inclusive Participation: Encourage inclusive participation, ensuring that all voices are heard and valued.

- Equal Contributions: Promote equal contributions by actively engaging quieter participants and managing dominant voices.

2. Encouraging Practical Solutions:

- Focus on Feasibility: Encourage participants to suggest practical and feasible solutions that can be realistically implemented.

- Consider Resources: Ensure that the proposed actions consider available resources and support systems.

3. Balancing Needs and Capabilities:

- Assess Needs: Ensure that the agreement addresses the needs of all participants, including victims, offenders, and the community.

- Evaluate Capabilities: Assess the capabilities of the offenders and other participants to fulfill their responsibilities within the agreement.

4. Ensuring Clarity and Specificity:

- Clear Actions: Clearly define each action, specifying what needs to be done, by whom, and by when.

- Detailed Responsibilities: Clearly outline the responsibilities of each participant, avoiding vague or ambiguous commitments.

5. Building Consensus:

- Facilitate Dialogue: Facilitate open and respectful dialogue to build consensus on the proposed actions.

- Seek Common Ground: Encourage participants to find common ground and work towards mutually acceptable solutions.

6. Establishing Accountability Mechanisms:

- Monitoring Progress: Establish mechanisms for monitoring progress and ensuring that commitments are honored.

- Providing Support: Offer support and resources to help participants fulfill their responsibilities and overcome any challenges.

Examples of Effective Agreements

Example 1: School-Based Restorative Justice Circle

In a high school, a restorative justice circle is convened to address a case of vandalism. The facilitator guides the participants through the agreement phase with the following approach:

1. Summarizing Key Points: The facilitator summarizes the impact of the vandalism on the school and the affected students.

2. Identifying Possible Actions: Participants brainstorm actions such as repairing the damaged property, community service, and educational workshops on respecting school property.

3. Building Consensus: The group reaches a consensus on a combination of actions, including restitution, a formal apology, and participation in a school beautification project.

4. Drafting the Agreement: The facilitator drafts the agreement, detailing the specific actions, responsibilities, and timelines.

5. Documenting the Agreement: The agreement is documented in writing and reviewed by all participants for approval.

6. Establishing Follow-Up: Follow-up meetings are scheduled to review progress and ensure accountability.

Example 2: Community Restorative Justice Circle

In a neighborhood affected by repeated noise disturbances, a restorative justice circle is held. The facilitator ensures an effective agreement with these steps:

1. Summarizing Key Points: The facilitator reviews the impact of the noise disturbances on the community's well-being and peace.

2. Identifying Possible Actions: Participants brainstorm solutions such as setting quiet hours, installing soundproofing, and organizing community events to build better relationships.

3. Building Consensus: The group agrees on implementing quiet hours, soundproofing measures for the offenders' homes, and organizing monthly community meetings.

4. Drafting the Agreement: The agreement is drafted, specifying the actions, responsible parties, and implementation timelines.

5. Documenting the Agreement: The written agreement is reviewed and approved by all participants.

6. Establishing Follow-Up: Regular follow-up meetings are scheduled to monitor compliance and address any ongoing concerns.

Conclusion

The agreement phase of a restorative justice circle is vital for reaching a consensus on how to repair the harm and prevent future occurrences. By fostering collaborative decision-making, encouraging practical solutions, and ensuring clarity and specificity, facilitators can guide participants towards meaningful and actionable agreements. Effective agreements promote accountability, healing, and community cohesion, creating a foundation for lasting positive change. Through thoughtful facilitation and adherence to established guidelines, the agreement phase can lead to successful outcomes that benefit all participants and the broader community.

Closing: Concluding with Reflections and a Closing Ritual

The closing phase of a restorative justice circle is essential for bringing the process to a meaningful and respectful conclusion. It allows participants to reflect on the experience, express final thoughts, and reinforce commitments made during the circle. A thoughtful closing, often involving a ritual, helps solidify the progress made and promotes a sense of closure and readiness to move forward. This chapter explores the importance of the closing phase, elements to include, and strategies for creating an effective and respectful conclusion to the circle.

The Importance of the Closing Phase

The closing phase serves several crucial functions:

1. Reflection and Integration: It provides an opportunity for participants to reflect on the discussions, integrate insights, and express how the process has affected them.

2. Reinforcement of Commitments: Reiterating agreements and commitments helps ensure that the actions decided upon are understood and taken seriously.

3. Emotional Closure: A thoughtful closing helps participants achieve emotional closure, reducing any lingering tension or unresolved feelings.

4. Community Bonding: Concluding with a ritual or shared activity strengthens the sense of community and mutual support.

5. Acknowledgement and Gratitude: It allows participants to express gratitude for each other's participation and contributions, fostering positive relationships.

Elements of an Effective Closing

An effective closing for a restorative justice circle can include several key elements:

1. Reflection:

- Personal Reflections: Invite participants to share their reflections on the circle process, what they learned, and how they feel.

- Facilitator's Reflection: The facilitator shares their own reflections and acknowledges the effort and courage of participants.

2. Reiteration of Agreements:

- Review of Agreements: Briefly review the agreements made during the circle, ensuring clarity and mutual understanding.

- Commitment Statements: Encourage participants to reaffirm their commitment to the agreed actions and responsibilities.

3. Closing Ritual:

- Cultural Practices: Incorporate cultural or traditional rituals relevant to the participants, such as a prayer, song, or blessing.

- Symbolic Actions: Use symbolic actions to signify the closing of the circle, such as extinguishing a candle or passing a symbolic object one last time.

4. Expression of Gratitude:

- Gratitude Statements: Allow participants to express gratitude to each other for their participation, honesty, and contributions.

- Acknowledgement of Efforts: The facilitator acknowledges the efforts and contributions of all participants.

5. Encouragement and Hope:

- Positive Affirmations: Share positive affirmations and words of encouragement to leave participants feeling hopeful and supported.

- Future Outlook: Discuss the next steps and express optimism for the future, reinforcing the positive impact of the circle.

Strategies for Creating an Effective Closing

Facilitators play a crucial role in guiding the closing phase. Here are some strategies for creating an effective and respectful conclusion:

1. Fostering Reflection:

- Open-Ended Questions: Use open-ended questions to invite reflections, such as "What is one thing you are taking away from today's circle?" or "How has this process impacted you?"

- Encouraging Honesty: Encourage participants to be honest in their reflections, validating all emotions and insights.

2. Reinforcing Agreements:

- Clear Summarization: Clearly summarize the agreements and commitments made, ensuring that everyone understands their roles.

- Written Reminders: Provide written reminders of the agreements to participants as a tangible reference.

3. Incorporating Rituals:

- Meaningful Rituals: Choose rituals that are meaningful to the group and relevant to the cultural or traditional context.

- Inclusive Practices: Ensure that the rituals are inclusive and respectful of all participants' beliefs and practices.

4. Expressing Gratitude:

- Modeling Gratitude: The facilitator models gratitude by thanking participants for their honesty, bravery, and contributions.

- Inviting Gratitude: Invite participants to express gratitude to each other, fostering a positive and supportive atmosphere.

5. Ending on a Positive Note:

- Encouraging Words: Share encouraging words and affirmations to leave participants feeling supported and optimistic.

- Future Connections: Emphasize the importance of staying connected and supporting each other beyond the circle.

Examples of Effective Closings

Example 1: School-Based Restorative Justice Circle

In a high school setting, a restorative justice circle addressing a conflict between students concludes with the following steps:

1. Reflection: The facilitator invites each student to share their reflections on the circle, what they have learned, and how they feel about the resolutions.

2. Reiteration of Agreements: The facilitator briefly reviews the agreements made, including apologies, restitution, and future behavior expectations.

3. Closing Ritual: The group participates in a symbolic action, such as writing down a positive commitment and placing it in a "commitment box."

4. Expression of Gratitude: Students and the facilitator express gratitude to each other for their honesty, participation, and willingness to resolve the conflict.

5. Encouragement and Hope: The facilitator shares words of encouragement, emphasizing the importance of continued respect and support within the school community.

Example 2: Community Restorative Justice Circle

In a neighborhood affected by vandalism, a restorative justice circle concludes with the following steps:

1. Reflection: Community members share their reflections on the impact of the circle and their hopes for the neighborhood moving forward.

2. Reiteration of Agreements: The facilitator reviews the agreed actions, including community service projects and preventive measures.

3. Closing Ritual: The group participates in a traditional blessing led by a community elder, symbolizing unity and healing.

4. Expression of Gratitude: Participants express gratitude to each other for their openness and commitment to improving the community.

5. Encouragement and Hope: The facilitator shares positive affirmations, emphasizing the potential for positive change and continued collaboration.

Conclusion

The closing phase of a restorative justice circle is vital for bringing the process to a meaningful and respectful conclusion. By incorporating elements of reflection, reiteration of agreements, closing rituals, and expressions of gratitude, facilitators can ensure that participants leave the circle feeling heard, validated, and hopeful. An effective closing reinforces the commitments made, fosters emotional closure, and strengthens the sense of community and mutual support. Thoughtful facilitation and adherence to established guidelines help create a positive and lasting impact, promoting healing and reconciliation beyond the circle.

CHAPTER 07

CASE STUDIES: SUCCESS STORIES FROM RESTORATIVE JUSTICE CIRCLES

Real-world examples demonstrate the effectiveness of restorative justice circles. This chapter presents case studies from various settings, showcasing the transformative impact of this approach on individuals and communities. These case studies highlight how restorative justice circles can address harm, foster healing, and build stronger, more cohesive communities.

Case Study 1: School-Based Restorative Justice Circle

Background

A high school experienced a significant increase in bullying incidents, particularly targeting a new student, Emily. The traditional disciplinary approach had not been effective in addressing the root causes of the behavior or fostering a supportive school environment. The school decided to implement a restorative justice circle to address the issue comprehensively.

Circle Process

Preparation:

- Individual meetings were held with Emily, the main offenders, and other affected students to explain the restorative justice process and address any concerns.

- Ground rules were established, emphasizing respect, active listening, and confidentiality.

Opening:

- The facilitator opened the circle with a welcoming statement, setting a positive and respectful tone.

- A moment of silence was observed to reflect on the importance of the process.

Sharing:

- Emily shared her experiences and the emotional impact the bullying had on her.

- The offenders took turns speaking, explaining their actions and the reasons behind their behavior.

- Other students shared how the bullying affected the school environment and their relationships.

Discussion:

- Participants explored the harm caused by the bullying and its broader impact on the school community.

- They discussed the underlying issues that led to the bullying behavior, such as peer pressure and lack of awareness about its effects.

Agreement:

- The group reached a consensus on several actions, including formal apologies to Emily, participation in anti-bullying workshops, and a peer support program.

- An action plan was developed, detailing specific responsibilities and timelines for each agreed action.

Closing:

- Participants shared their reflections on the circle process and expressed gratitude for each other's honesty and participation.

- The circle concluded with a symbolic gesture of unity, such as linking arms and making a commitment to a supportive school environment.

Outcome

The restorative justice circle led to significant positive changes within the school:

- Emily felt heard, validated, and supported by her peers.

- The offenders gained a deeper understanding of the impact of their actions and took responsibility for making amends.

- The anti-bullying workshops and peer support program fostered a more inclusive and respectful school culture.

- Follow-up meetings confirmed sustained improvements in behavior and relationships among students.

Case Study 2: Community Restorative Justice Circle

Background

In a neighborhood struggling with repeated incidents of vandalism, residents felt unsafe and disconnected. Traditional punitive measures had not resolved the issue or addressed the underlying causes. A community restorative justice circle was organized to address the harm and rebuild trust.

Circle Process

Preparation:

- Facilitators held individual meetings with affected residents, offenders, and community leaders to explain the process and gather input.

- Participants agreed on ground rules focused on respectful communication and confidentiality.

Opening:

- The circle began with a welcoming statement from the facilitator, emphasizing the goal of healing and community restoration.

- A local elder led a traditional blessing to honor the community's cultural heritage.

Sharing:

- Residents shared their experiences of the vandalism and its impact on their sense of safety and community spirit.

- Offenders explained their motivations and circumstances that led to their actions.

- Community leaders discussed the broader implications for the neighborhood and the importance of collective responsibility.

Discussion:

- The discussion focused on understanding the harm caused and identifying underlying issues such as lack of recreational activities for youth and social disconnection.

- Participants brainstormed potential solutions to address these root causes and repair the harm.

Agreement:

- The group reached an agreement on several actions: organizing community cleanup events, creating youth recreational programs, and establishing a neighborhood watch.

- An action plan was created, outlining specific tasks, responsible individuals, and timelines for implementation.

Closing:

- Participants reflected on the process, shared their hopes for the future and expressed gratitude for each other's contributions.

- The circle concluded with a community meal, reinforcing the sense of unity and mutual support.

Outcome

The community restorative justice circle resulted in significant positive changes:

- The cleanup events restored the physical appearance of the neighborhood, enhancing residents' sense of pride and ownership.

- The youth recreational programs provided constructive activities, reducing the likelihood of future vandalism.

- The neighborhood watch improved safety and fostered stronger connections among residents.

- Follow-up meetings demonstrated sustained engagement and continued efforts to build a cohesive and supportive community.

Case Study 3: Workplace Restorative Justice Circle

Background

A workplace experiences ongoing conflicts between employees, leading to a toxic environment and decreased productivity. Traditional HR interventions had not effectively resolved the underlying issues. A restorative justice circle was implemented to address the conflicts and promote a healthier workplace culture.

Circle Process

Preparation:

- Individual meetings were conducted with employees involved in the conflicts and other affected staff members to explain the process and gather input.

- Ground rules were established, emphasizing respect, confidentiality, and a commitment to positive change.

Opening:

- The facilitator opened the circle with a welcoming statement, highlighting the goal of resolving conflicts and improving the workplace environment.

- A moment of silence was observed to reflect on the importance of the process.

Sharing:

- Employees shared their experiences of the conflicts and their impact on their work and well-being.

- Participants took turns speaking, discussing their perspectives and underlying issues contributing to the conflicts.

Discussion:

- The discussion focused on understanding the harm caused by the conflicts and identifying underlying issues such as communication breakdowns, workload stress, and lack of team cohesion.

- Participants brainstormed potential solutions to address these issues and improve workplace relationships.

Agreement:

- The group reached an agreement on several actions: implementing regular team-building activities, establishing clear communication channels, and providing stress management resources.

- An action plan was developed, detailing specific responsibilities and timelines for each agreed action.

Closing:

- Participants reflected on the process, shared their commitments to positive change and expressed gratitude for each other's honesty and participation.

- The circle concluded with a symbolic gesture, such as a group handshake or shared commitment to a healthier workplace culture.

Outcome

The workplace restorative justice circle led to significant positive changes:

- Employees felt heard, validated, and more connected to their colleagues.

- The team-building activities and improved communication channels fostered a more collaborative and supportive work environment.

- Stress management resources helped employees cope with workload pressures, reducing conflict and improving overall well-being.

- Follow-up meetings confirmed sustained improvements in workplace relationships and productivity.

Conclusion

These case studies highlight the transformative impact of restorative justice circles in various settings, demonstrating their effectiveness in addressing harm, fostering healing, and building stronger communities. By providing a structured and respectful space for dialogue, restorative justice circles empower participants to take responsibility, develop empathy, and collaboratively seek solutions. The success stories from schools, communities, and workplaces showcase the potential of this approach to create meaningful and lasting positive change.

CHAPTER 08

CHALLENGES AND SOLUTIONS IN RESTORATIVE JUSTICE CIRCLES

While restorative justice circles can be highly effective, they also present challenges that must be addressed to ensure their success. This chapter identifies common obstacles, such as resistance from participants, cultural barriers, and logistical issues, and offers strategies for overcoming them. Understanding and addressing these challenges can enhance the effectiveness and sustainability of restorative justice circles.

Common Challenges in Restorative Justice Circles

1. Resistance from Participants:

- Reluctance to Participate: Some individuals may be reluctant to participate in the circle process due to fear, mistrust, or skepticism about its effectiveness.

- Denial of Responsibility: Offenders may deny their responsibility for the harm, making it difficult to achieve genuine accountability and healing.

2. Cultural Barriers:

- Cultural Differences: Participants from diverse cultural backgrounds may have different communication styles, values, and expectations that can affect their engagement in the circle.

- Language Barriers: Language differences can hinder effective communication and understanding among participants.

3. Emotional Intensity:

- Managing Strong Emotions: The circle process can evoke strong emotions, such as anger, sadness, or shame, which can be challenging to manage.

- Risk of Re-Traumatization: Victims or offenders with past trauma may experience re-traumatization during the circle process.

4. Power Imbalances:

- Unequal Participation: Power imbalances among participants, such as differences in social status, authority, or confidence, can affect the fairness and inclusivity of the process.

- Dominant Voices: Some participants may dominate the discussion, while others may feel marginalized or silenced.

5. Logistical Issues:

- Scheduling Conflicts: Finding a suitable time and place for the circle that accommodates all participants can be challenging.

- Resource Limitations: Limited resources, such as trained facilitators, funding, or materials, can hinder the implementation and sustainability of restorative justice circles.

Strategies for Overcoming Challenges

1. Addressing Resistance from Participants:

- Building Trust and Rapport: Facilitators should focus on building trust and rapport with participants through empathy, active listening, and respect.

- Education and Awareness: Providing education about the principles and benefits of restorative justice can help alleviate skepticism and encourage participation.

- Encouraging Voluntary Participation: Emphasize the voluntary nature of the process and respect individuals' choices to participate or not.

2. Navigating Cultural Barriers:

- Cultural Sensitivity Training: Facilitators should receive training on cultural sensitivity to understand and respect diverse cultural backgrounds and practices.

- Inclusive Practices: Incorporate inclusive practices that honor participants' cultural traditions and values within the circle process.

- Language Support: Provide language support, such as interpreters or translated materials, to facilitate effective communication.

3. Managing Emotional Intensity:

- Creating a Safe Space: Establish a safe and supportive environment where participants feel comfortable expressing their emotions.

- Emotional Support Resources: Provide access to emotional support resources, such as counseling or peer support, for participants who need additional help.

- Grounding Techniques: Use grounding techniques, such as mindfulness exercises or breaks, to help participants manage strong emotions during the circle.

4. Addressing Power Imbalances:

- Equalizing Participation: Encourage equal participation by actively inviting quieter members to share their perspectives and managing dominant voices.

- Empowerment Strategies: Empower marginalized participants by validating their experiences and ensuring their voices are heard.

- Facilitator Interventions: Facilitators should be prepared to intervene if power imbalances disrupt the fairness and inclusivity of the process.

5. Overcoming Logistical Issues:

- Flexible Scheduling: Offer flexible scheduling options to accommodate participants' availability and commitments.

- Resource Mobilization: Mobilize resources from various sectors, such as community organizations, government agencies, or private donors, to support the implementation and sustainability of restorative justice circles.

- Leveraging Technology: Utilize technology, such as virtual meetings, to facilitate participation when in-person gatherings are not feasible.

Case Examples of Overcoming Challenges

Case Example 1: Addressing Resistance in a School Setting

Challenge: In a high school, some students were reluctant to participate in a restorative justice circle addressing bullying due to fear of retaliation and skepticism about the process.

Solution:

- Building Trust: The facilitator held individual meetings with the reluctant students to build trust, explain the process, and address their concerns.

- Peer Support: Peer mentors who had previously participated in restorative justice circles shared their positive experiences, encouraging reluctant students to participate.

- Voluntary Participation: Emphasizing the voluntary nature of the process, the facilitator reassured students that their participation was their choice.

Outcome:

- Reluctant students decided to participate after understanding the process and feeling supported.

- The circle successfully addressed the bullying, leading to improved relationships and a more inclusive school environment.

Case Example 2: Navigating Cultural Barriers in a Community Setting

Challenge: In a diverse neighborhood, cultural differences and language barriers hindered effective communication and engagement in a restorative justice circle addressing community conflicts.

Solution:

- Cultural Sensitivity Training: Facilitators received training on cultural sensitivity to understand and respect the diverse backgrounds of participants.

- Inclusive Practices: The circle incorporated cultural practices, such as traditional blessings and rituals, to honor participants' cultural values.

- Language Support: Interpreters were provided to facilitate communication for participants who did not speak the primary language.

Outcome:

- Participants felt respected and valued, leading to more open and effective communication.

- The circle successfully addressed the conflicts, fostering a stronger sense of community and mutual respect.

Case Example 3: Managing Emotional Intensity in a Workplace Setting

Challenge: In a workplace restorative justice circle addressing conflicts between employees, strong emotions, such as anger and frustration, were challenging to manage.

Solution:

- Creating a Safe Space: The facilitator established a safe and supportive environment, emphasizing respect and confidentiality.

- Emotional Support Resources: Counseling services were made available to employees who needed additional emotional support.

- Grounding Techniques: The facilitator used grounding techniques, such as guided breathing exercises and breaks, to help participants manage their emotions.

Outcome:

- Participants felt safe expressing their emotions, leading to more honest and productive discussions.

- The circle successfully resolved the conflicts, improving workplace relationships and overall well-being.

Conclusion

Restorative justice circles can be highly effective in addressing harm, fostering healing, and building stronger communities, but they also present challenges that must be navigated thoughtfully. By understanding common obstacles, such as resistance from participants, cultural barriers, emotional intensity, power imbalances, and logistical issues, facilitators can develop strategies to overcome these challenges and enhance the effectiveness of the circle process. Through trust-building, cultural sensitivity, emotional support, equal participation, and resource mobilization, restorative justice circles can achieve their transformative potential, promoting accountability, empathy, and reconciliation in diverse settings.

CHAPTER 09

THE PSYCHOLOGICAL AND EMOTIONAL IMPACT OF RESTORATIVE JUSTICE

Restorative justice circles can have profound psychological and emotional effects on participants. These impacts can be both beneficial and challenging, affecting victims, offenders, and community members in various ways. This chapter explores the psychological and emotional benefits of restorative justice circles, such as increased empathy and reduced recidivism, as well as potential risks and strategies for addressing them.

Psychological and Emotional Benefits

Restorative justice circles offer several psychological and emotional benefits for participants:

1. Increased Empathy:

- Understanding Others' Perspectives: By sharing and listening to personal stories, participants develop a deeper understanding of each other's experiences and emotions.

- Building Emotional Connections: The process fosters emotional connections between victims, offenders, and community members, enhancing empathy and compassion.

2. Reduced Recidivism:

- Accountability and Reflection: Offenders who participate in restorative justice circles are encouraged to take responsibility for their actions and reflect on the impact of their behavior, reducing the likelihood of reoffending.

- Positive Behavioral Change: The process promotes positive behavioral change by addressing the underlying causes of the harm and supporting personal growth.

3. Healing and Closure:

- Emotional Expression: Participants have the opportunity to express their emotions, including anger, sadness, and forgiveness, which can be cathartic and healing.

- Resolution of Conflict: Reaching agreements and making amends helps participants achieve a sense of closure, reducing lingering negative emotions.

4. Enhanced Self-Esteem and Empowerment:

- Voice and Agency: Victims and community members feel empowered by having a voice in the process and contributing to the resolution.

- Restored Dignity: Offenders who take responsibility and make amends can restore their sense of dignity and self-worth.

5. Strengthened Community Bonds:

- Collective Healing: The process promotes collective healing and strengthens community bonds by addressing harm and fostering mutual support.

- Improved Relationships: Participants often leave the circle with improved relationships and a renewed sense of trust and solidarity.

Potential Risks and Challenges

While restorative justice circles offer many benefits, they also present potential psychological and emotional risks:

1. Re-Traumatization:

- Emotional Intensity: The process can evoke strong emotions and memories of the harm, potentially re-traumatizing victims or offenders with past trauma.

- Unresolved Trauma: Participants with unresolved trauma may struggle to engage fully in the process or experience heightened emotional distress.

2. Resistance and Denial:

- Denial of Responsibility: Offenders who deny responsibility or show resistance to the process can hinder the effectiveness of the circle and exacerbate tensions.

- Lack of Participation: Participants who are unwilling or unable to engage meaningfully can disrupt the process and impact the outcomes.

3. Power Imbalances:

- Dominance and Marginalization: Power imbalances among participants, such as differences in social status or authority, can affect the fairness and inclusivity of the process.

- Intimidation and Silence: Victims or less assertive participants may feel intimidated or silenced by more dominant voices.

4. Emotional Burnout:

- Facilitator Burnout: Facilitators may experience emotional burnout due to the intensity and frequency of managing restorative justice circles.

- Participant Burnout: Participants may also experience emotional exhaustion if the process is particularly intense or prolonged.

Strategies for Addressing Psychological and Emotional Risks

To mitigate potential risks and enhance the psychological and emotional benefits of restorative justice circles, facilitators and organizers can implement several strategies:

1. Creating a Safe and Supportive Environment:

- Establishing Ground Rules: Set clear ground rules for respectful communication, confidentiality, and non-violence to create a safe space for participants.

- Providing Emotional Support: Ensure access to emotional support resources, such as counseling or peer support, for participants who need additional help.

2. Facilitator Training and Support:

- Comprehensive Training: Provide facilitators with comprehensive training on managing emotional intensity, recognizing signs of trauma, and addressing power imbalances.

- Regular Supervision: Offer regular supervision and support for facilitators to help them manage emotional burnout and maintain their well-being.

3. Trauma-Informed Practices:

- Recognizing Trauma: Train facilitators to recognize signs of trauma and implement trauma-informed practices to support affected participants.

- Providing Safe Alternatives: Offer alternative restorative practices or support services for participants who may not be ready for the circle process due to trauma.

4. Encouraging Voluntary Participation:

- Emphasizing Choice: Emphasize the voluntary nature of the process and respect participants' choices to engage or not engage in the circle.

- Building Trust: Focus on building trust and rapport with participants through empathy, active listening, and respect.

5. Balancing Power Dynamics:

- Equalizing Participation: Actively encourage equal participation by inviting quieter members to share their perspectives and managing dominant voices.

- Empowering Marginalized Voices: Empower marginalized participants by validating their experiences and ensuring their voices are heard.

6. Facilitating Emotional Expression and Reflection:

- Guided Reflection: Use guided reflection and mindfulness exercises to help participants process their emotions and experiences.

- Creating Opportunities for Closure: Provide opportunities for participants to achieve emotional closure, such as through rituals or symbolic actions.

Case Examples of Psychological and Emotional Impact

Case Example 1: Increased Empathy and Reduced Recidivism

Scenario: In a juvenile detention center, restorative justice circles were implemented to address conflicts between young offenders and their victims.

Outcome:

- Increased Empathy: Offenders developed a deeper understanding of the impact of their actions on their victims, fostering empathy and remorse.

- Reduced Recidivism: Follow-up studies showed a significant reduction in reoffending rates among participants, attributed to the accountability and reflection encouraged by the circles.

Case Example 2: Healing and Closure in a Community Setting

Scenario: A restorative justice circle was held in a community affected by a series of burglaries, involving victims, offenders, and community members.

Outcome:

- Healing and Closure: Victims felt heard and validated, achieving a sense of closure through the offenders' sincere apologies and reparative actions.

- Strengthened Community Bonds: The process fostered collective healing and strengthened community bonds, with participants reporting improved relationships and trust.

Case Example 3: Managing Emotional Intensity in a School Setting

Scenario: A high school restorative justice circle addressed bullying incidents, involving the victims, offenders, and other affected students.

Outcome:

- Emotional Expression: Participants were able to express their emotions, including anger and forgiveness, in a safe and supportive environment.

- Positive Behavioral Change: Offenders showed positive behavioral changes, supported by follow-up counseling and peer support programs.

Conclusion

Restorative justice circles can have profound psychological and emotional impacts on participants, offering benefits such as increased empathy, reduced recidivism, healing, and strengthened community bonds. However, they also present potential risks, including re-traumatization, resistance, power imbalances, and emotional burnout. By implementing strategies to create a safe and supportive environment, providing facilitator training and support, using trauma-informed practices, and balancing power dynamics, facilitators can enhance the benefits and mitigate the risks. Through thoughtful facilitation and a focus on psychological and emotional well-being, restorative justice circles can achieve their transformative potential, promoting healing, accountability, and reconciliation for individuals and communities.

CHAPTER 10

RESTORATIVE JUSTICE CIRCLES IN SCHOOLS

Schools are increasingly adopting restorative justice circles to address conflicts and build positive environments. This chapter examines how circles can be used to resolve disputes, improve student behavior, and create a supportive school culture. By integrating restorative justice principles into the school setting, educators can foster a sense of community, accountability, and mutual respect among students and staff.

The Role of Restorative Justice Circles in Schools

Restorative justice circles in schools serve multiple purposes:

1. Conflict Resolution: Circles provide a structured and respectful environment for students to address and resolve conflicts.

2. Behavior Improvement: The process encourages students to reflect on their behavior, understand its impact, and take responsibility for their actions.

3. Community Building: Circles promote a sense of community and mutual support, enhancing relationships among students, teachers, and staff.

4. Emotional Support: The process offers emotional support and a safe space for students to express their feelings and experiences.

5. Prevention and Education: Restorative justice circles educate students about the principles of respect, empathy, and accountability, helping to prevent future conflicts.

Implementing Restorative Justice Circles in Schools

Successful implementation of restorative justice circles in schools involves several key steps:

1. Building Awareness and Support:

- Educating Stakeholders: Educate students, teachers, administrators, and parents about the principles and benefits of restorative justice.

- Gaining Buy-In: Build support among all stakeholders by highlighting success stories and demonstrating the positive impact of restorative justice circles.

2. Training Facilitators:

- Comprehensive Training: Provide comprehensive training for facilitators, including teachers, counselors, and peer leaders, on the principles and practices of restorative justice.

- Ongoing Professional Development: Offer ongoing professional development opportunities to enhance facilitators' skills and knowledge.

3. Establishing Clear Procedures:

- Developing Guidelines: Create clear guidelines for conducting restorative justice circles, including ground rules, roles, and responsibilities.

- Consistent Implementation: Ensure consistent implementation of circles across the school, with support from administrators and staff.

4. Creating a Safe and Inclusive Environment:

- Establishing Ground Rules: Set and enforce ground rules for respectful communication, confidentiality, and non-violence.

- Promoting Inclusivity: Ensure that the circle process is inclusive and respectful of all students' cultural backgrounds and perspectives.

5. Integrating Circles into School Culture:

- Regular Practice: Integrate restorative justice circles into the regular practices of the school, using them for both conflict resolution and community building.

- Embedding Principles: Embed the principles of restorative justice into the school's policies, curriculum, and disciplinary procedures.

Applications of Restorative Justice Circles in Schools

Restorative justice circles can be applied in various contexts within schools:

1. Addressing Bullying and Conflicts:

- Conflict Resolution Circles: Use circles to address specific incidents of bullying or conflicts between students, allowing them to share their perspectives, understand the impact, and develop mutually agreed-upon resolutions.

- Prevention Programs: Implement regular circles focused on bullying prevention and promoting a culture of respect and inclusion.

2. Improving Student Behavior:

- Reflective Circles: Use circles as a tool for students to reflect on their behavior, understand its impact on others, and develop strategies for positive change.

- Accountability Circles: Hold students accountable for their actions by involving them in circles where they can make amends and restore relationships.

3. Building a Supportive School Culture:

- Community Building Circles: Conduct regular community-building circles to strengthen relationships, foster a sense of belonging, and promote mutual support among students and staff.

- Cultural Celebrations: Use circles to celebrate cultural diversity and promote inclusivity, allowing students to share their cultural backgrounds and experiences.

4. Providing Emotional Support:

- Support Circles: Create support circles for students experiencing personal challenges, providing a safe space for them to share their feelings and receive support from peers and staff.

- Crisis Response: Use circles to support students and staff in the aftermath of a crisis or traumatic event, promoting healing and resilience.

Case Studies of Restorative Justice Circles in Schools

Case Study 1: Addressing Bullying in a Middle School

Background: A middle school experienced ongoing bullying incidents, creating a hostile environment for several students. Traditional disciplinary measures were not effective in resolving the issue or supporting the victims.

Implementation:

- Conflict Resolution Circles: The school implemented restorative justice circles to address specific bullying incidents. Facilitators held individual meetings with the victims and offenders to prepare them for the circle.

- Circle Process: During the circles, victims shared their experiences and the impact of the bullying on their lives. Offenders were encouraged to take responsibility for their actions and understand the harm they caused.

- Agreements: The circles resulted in agreements for the offenders to apologize, participate in bullying prevention workshops, and engage in community service within the school.

Outcome:

- Reduced Bullying: The frequency of bullying incidents decreased significantly, and the school environment became more positive and inclusive.

- Improved Relationships: Relationships between students improved, with increased empathy and understanding among peers.

- Supportive Culture: The school's culture shifted towards greater support and respect, with ongoing circles reinforcing these values.

Case Study 2: Improving Behavior in a High School

Background: A high school faced challenges with student behavior, including frequent conflicts and disciplinary issues. The administration sought an alternative approach to traditional punitive measures.

Implementation:

- Reflective Circles: The school introduced reflective circles for students who had committed disciplinary infractions. These circles allowed students to reflect on their behavior, understand its impact, and develop strategies for improvement.

- Accountability Circles: For more serious infractions, accountability circles were held, involving the affected parties, facilitators, and school staff. Students were encouraged to take responsibility and make amends.

Outcome:

- Behavioral Improvement: Students participating in the circles showed significant behavioral improvement, with reduced repeat offenses.

- Increased Accountability: The process fostered a sense of accountability among students, leading to more thoughtful and responsible behavior.

- Positive School Climate: The overall school climate improved, with fewer conflicts and a greater sense of community and mutual respect.

Case Study 3: Building Community in an Elementary School

Background: An elementary school sought to strengthen community bonds and promote a supportive environment for students and staff.

Implementation:

- Community Building Circles: The school conducted regular community-building circles, bringing together students, teachers, and staff to share their experiences, celebrate achievements, and discuss common goals.

- Cultural Celebrations: Circles were used to celebrate cultural diversity, allowing students to share their cultural backgrounds and learn from each other.

Outcome:

- Enhanced Sense of Belonging: Students and staff reported a stronger sense of belonging and connection to the school community.

- Positive Relationships: Relationships among students, teachers, and staff improved, with increased trust and mutual support.

- Inclusive Environment: The school environment became more inclusive and respectful, with a greater appreciation for cultural diversity.

Conclusion

Restorative justice circles offer a powerful tool for schools to address conflicts, improve student behavior, and create a supportive and inclusive environment. By implementing circles for conflict resolution, behavior improvement, community building, and emotional support, schools can foster a culture of empathy, accountability, and mutual respect. Through thoughtful planning, comprehensive training, and consistent application, restorative justice circles can transform school communities, promoting positive relationships and enhancing the overall educational experience for students and staff.

CHAPTER 11

RESTORATIVE JUSTICE CIRCLES IN THE WORKPLACE

Workplace conflicts can disrupt productivity and morale, leading to a toxic environment and reduced job satisfaction. Restorative justice circles offer a structured and respectful approach to addressing grievances, improving communication, and fostering a collaborative culture in professional settings. This chapter explores how restorative justice circles can be effectively applied in workplaces to resolve conflicts, build stronger relationships, and enhance overall workplace harmony.

The Role of Restorative Justice Circles in the Workplace

Restorative justice circles in the workplace serve multiple purposes:

1. Conflict Resolution: Circles provide a platform for employees to address and resolve conflicts constructively.

2. Improved Communication: The process encourages open and honest communication, helping to break down barriers and misunderstandings.

3. Relationship Building: Circles foster stronger relationships among colleagues by promoting empathy, respect, and mutual support.

4. Enhancing Collaboration: The process builds a collaborative culture where employees work together to find solutions and support each other.

5. Promoting Accountability: Circles encourage accountability by allowing employees to take responsibility for their actions and their impact on others.

Implementing Restorative Justice Circles in the Workplace

Successful implementation of restorative justice circles in the workplace involves several key steps:

1. Building Awareness and Support:

- Educating Employees: Provide information and training about the principles and benefits of restorative justice to all employees.

- Gaining Buy-In: Secure support from leadership and staff by demonstrating the positive impact of restorative justice on workplace culture.

2. Training Facilitators:

- Comprehensive Training: Train facilitators, such as HR professionals or designated staff members, in restorative justice principles and practices.

- Ongoing Development: Offer ongoing professional development opportunities to enhance facilitators' skills and knowledge.

3. Establishing Clear Procedures:

- Developing Guidelines: Create clear guidelines for conducting restorative justice circles, including ground rules, roles, and responsibilities.

- Consistent Implementation: Ensure consistent application of circles across the organization with support from management.

4. Creating a Safe and Inclusive Environment:

- Establishing Ground Rules: Set and enforce ground rules for respectful communication, confidentiality, and non-violence.

- Promoting Inclusivity: Ensure that the circle process is inclusive and respectful of all employees' perspectives.

5. Integrating Circles into Workplace Culture:

- Regular Practice: Integrate restorative justice circles into regular workplace practices for conflict resolution and team building.

- Embedding Principles: Embed restorative justice principles into the organization's policies, procedures, and culture.

Applications of Restorative Justice Circles in the Workplace

Restorative justice circles can be applied in various contexts within the workplace:

1. Addressing Grievances and Conflicts:

- Conflict Resolution Circles: Use circles to address specific conflicts or grievances between employees, allowing them to share their perspectives, understand the impact, and develop mutually agreed-upon resolutions.

- Prevention Programs: Implement regular circles focused on conflict prevention and promoting a culture of respect and collaboration.

2. Improving Communication:

- Reflective Circles: Use circles as a tool for employees to reflect on their communication styles, understand their impact, and develop strategies for improvement.

- Feedback Circles: Conduct circles where employees can give and receive constructive feedback in a supportive environment.

3. Building a Collaborative Culture:

- Team Building Circles: Conduct regular team-building circles to strengthen relationships, foster a sense of belonging, and promote mutual support among colleagues.

- Cultural Celebrations: Use circles to celebrate diversity and promote inclusivity, allowing employees to share their cultural backgrounds and experiences.

4. Providing Emotional Support:

- Support Circles: Create support circles for employees experiencing personal or professional challenges, providing a safe space for them to share their feelings and receive support.

- Crisis Response: Use circles to support employees in the aftermath of a crisis or traumatic event, promoting healing and resilience.

Case Studies of Restorative Justice Circles in the Workplace

Case Study 1: Addressing Workplace Conflict

Background: A mid-sized company faced ongoing conflicts between two departments, leading to a hostile work environment and decreased productivity. Traditional HR interventions have not been effective in resolving the issues.

Implementation:

- Conflict Resolution Circles: The company implemented restorative justice circles to address specific conflicts between the departments. Facilitators held individual meetings with the involved employees to prepare them for the circle.

- Circle Process: During the circles, employees shared their experiences and the impact of the conflicts on their work and well-being. They were encouraged to understand each other's perspectives and take responsibility for their actions.

- Agreements: The circles resulted in agreements for improved communication protocols, joint team-building activities, and regular check-ins to monitor progress.

Outcome:

- Reduced Conflict: The frequency and intensity of conflicts decreased significantly, and the work environment became more collaborative and supportive.

- Improved Relationships: Relationships between the departments improved, with increased empathy and understanding among colleagues.

- Enhanced Productivity: The overall productivity of the company improved as a result of reduced conflicts and better communication.

Case Study 2: Improving Communication in a Corporate Setting

Background: A large corporation experienced communication breakdowns and misunderstandings between management and staff, leading to frustration and decreased morale.

Implementation:

- Reflective Circles: The corporation introduced reflective circles for employees to reflect on their communication styles and their impact on their colleagues. These circles allowed employees to discuss challenges and develop strategies for improvement.

- Feedback Circles: Regular feedback circles were conducted, providing a platform for employees to give and receive constructive feedback in a supportive environment.

Outcome:

- Enhanced Communication: Employees reported improved communication and reduced misunderstandings, leading to a more cohesive work environment.

- Increased Morale: Employee morale improved as a result of the open and respectful communication fostered by the circles.

- Better Management-Staff Relationships: Relationships between management and staff improved, with increased trust and collaboration.

Case Study 3: Building a Collaborative Culture in a Non-Profit Organization

Background: A non-profit organization sought to strengthen its collaborative culture and promote mutual support among its diverse staff.

Implementation:

- Team Building Circles: The organization conducted regular team-building circles, bringing together staff members to share their experiences, celebrate achievements, and discuss common goals.

- Cultural Celebrations: Circles were used to celebrate cultural diversity, allowing employees to share their cultural backgrounds and learn from each other.

Outcome:

- Enhanced Sense of Belonging: Staff members reported a stronger sense of belonging and connection to the organization.

- Positive Relationships: Relationships among staff improved, with increased trust and mutual support.

- Inclusive Environment: The organization's environment became more inclusive and respectful, with a greater appreciation for cultural diversity.

Conclusion

Restorative justice circles offer a powerful tool for workplaces to address conflicts, improve communication, and create a collaborative and supportive environment. By implementing circles for conflict resolution, communication improvement, team building, and emotional support, organizations can foster a culture of empathy, accountability, and mutual respect. Through thoughtful planning, comprehensive training, and consistent application, restorative justice circles can transform workplace dynamics, enhancing productivity, morale, and overall job satisfaction for employees.

CHAPTER 12

RESTORATIVE JUSTICE CIRCLES IN THE CRIMINAL JUSTICE SYSTEM

Restorative justice circles offer a transformative alternative to traditional punitive measures within the criminal justice system. These circles focus on repairing harm, fostering accountability, and supporting the rehabilitation of offenders. This chapter explores the application of restorative justice circles in various contexts, such as juvenile justice, and their potential to reduce recidivism and support rehabilitation.

The Role of Restorative Justice Circles in the Criminal Justice System

Restorative justice circles serve several important functions within the criminal justice system:

1. Repairing Harm: Circles provide a space for victims, offenders, and community members to discuss the harm

caused by a crime and collaboratively develop a plan to repair it.

2. Fostering Accountability: Offenders are encouraged to take responsibility for their actions, understand the impact of their behavior, and make amends.

3. Supporting Rehabilitation: The process supports offenders' rehabilitation by addressing the underlying causes of their behavior and promoting personal growth.

4. Reducing Recidivism: By fostering empathy, accountability, and community support, restorative justice circles have the potential to reduce reoffending rates.

5. Empowering Victims: Victims are given a voice in the justice process, helping them to feel heard, validated, and supported.

Implementing Restorative Justice Circles in the Criminal Justice System

Successful implementation of restorative justice circles within the criminal justice system involves several key steps:

1. Building Awareness and Support:

- Educating Stakeholders: Provide education and training for judges, prosecutors, defense attorneys, probation officers, and community members about the principles and benefits of restorative justice.

- Gaining Buy-In: Secure support from key stakeholders by highlighting success stories and demonstrating the positive impact of restorative justice circles on reducing recidivism and supporting rehabilitation.

2. Training Facilitators:

- Comprehensive Training: Train facilitators, including justice system professionals and community volunteers, in restorative justice principles and practices.

- Ongoing Development: Offer ongoing professional development opportunities to enhance facilitators' skills and knowledge.

3. Establishing Clear Procedures:

- Developing Guidelines: Create clear guidelines for conducting restorative justice circles, including ground rules, roles, and responsibilities.

- Consistent Implementation: Ensure consistent application of circles across the justice system with support from judges, prosecutors, and defense attorneys.

4. Creating a Safe and Inclusive Environment:

- Establishing Ground Rules: Set and enforce ground rules for respectful communication, confidentiality, and non-violence.

- Promoting Inclusivity: Ensure that the circle process is inclusive and respectful of all participants' perspectives.

5. Integrating Circles into Justice Processes:

- Diversion Programs: Use restorative justice circles as a diversionary measure, offering an alternative to formal court proceedings for certain offenses.

- Sentencing Options: Integrate circles into sentencing options, allowing offenders to participate in restorative justice as part of their sentence.

Applications of Restorative Justice Circles in the Criminal Justice System

Restorative justice circles can be applied in various contexts within the criminal justice system:

1. Juvenile Justice:

- Diversion Programs: Implement circles as part of diversion programs for juvenile offenders, offering an alternative to formal court proceedings and incarceration.

- Rehabilitation Support: Use circles to support the rehabilitation of juvenile offenders, addressing underlying issues such as trauma, substance abuse, and family dynamics.

2. Adult Criminal Justice:

- Pre-Sentencing Circles: Conduct circles before sentencing to allow offenders to take responsibility, hear from victims, and develop a plan to repair the harm.

- Post-Sentencing Circles: Use circles as part of probation or parole conditions to support offenders' reintegration into the community and reduce recidivism.

3. Community-Based Justice:

- Community Circles: Engage community members in the circle process to address the broader impact of crime and promote collective healing and safety.

- Restorative Conferencing: Use restorative conferencing circles to address conflicts and crimes that affect entire communities, fostering collaborative solutions and community resilience.

Case Studies of Restorative Justice Circles in the Criminal Justice System

Case Study 1: Juvenile Justice Diversion Program

Background: The juvenile justice system faced high rates of recidivism among young offenders. Traditional punitive measures were not effective in addressing the root causes of their behavior.

Implementation:

- Diversionary Circles: The system implemented restorative justice circles as part of a diversion program for first-time and non-violent juvenile offenders. Facilitators held individual meetings with the offenders, victims, and their families to prepare them for the circle.

- Circle Process: During the circles, offenders shared their experiences and the impact of their actions. Victims described how the crime affected them. The group collaboratively developed a plan to repair the harm and support the offender's rehabilitation.

- Agreements: The circles resulted in agreements for restitution, community service, participation in counseling, and educational support.

Outcome:

- Reduced Recidivism: The recidivism rates among participants in the diversion program decreased significantly.

- Improved Rehabilitation: Juvenile offenders showed positive behavioral changes and improved relationships with their families and communities.

- Victim Satisfaction: Victims reported high levels of satisfaction with the process, feeling heard and validated.

Case Study 2: Pre-Sentencing Circles in Adult Criminal Justice

Background: An adult criminal justice system sought to integrate restorative justice principles into its sentencing practices to promote accountability and reduce reoffending.

Implementation:

- Pre-Sentencing Circles: The system introduced pre-sentencing restorative justice circles for eligible offenders. Facilitators prepared offenders, victims, and community members for the circle process.

- Circle Process: In the circles, offenders took responsibility for their actions, victims shared the impact of the crime, and the group discussed ways to repair the harm. The outcomes of the circles were considered in the sentencing decisions.

- Agreements: The circles resulted in agreements for restitution, community service, participation in rehabilitation programs, and victim-offender mediation.

Outcome:

- Enhanced Accountability: Offenders showed greater accountability for their actions and commitment to making amends.

- Reduced Recidivism: The recidivism rates among participants in the pre-sentencing circles were lower compared to those who went through traditional sentencing alone.

- Victim Empowerment: Victims felt empowered by having a voice in the justice process and contributing to the resolution.

Case Study 3: Community Circles for Addressing Crime

Background: A community experienced a series of property crimes that created fear and tension among residents. Traditional law enforcement responses were not addressing the community's need for safety and healing.

Implementation:

- Community Circles: The community, in collaboration with local law enforcement and restorative justice facilitators, implemented community circles to address the crimes and their impact. Facilitators prepared offenders, victims, and community members for the circle process.

- Circle Process: During the circles, offenders took responsibility for their actions, victims shared the impact on their lives, and community members discussed the broader effects on the neighborhood. The group collaboratively developed solutions to repair the harm and improve community safety.

- Agreements: The circles resulted in agreements for restitution, community service projects, neighborhood watch programs, and ongoing community meetings to address safety concerns.

Outcome:

- Community Healing: The circles facilitated collective healing and strengthened community bonds.

- Improved Safety: The implementation of community-based safety measures, such as neighborhood watch programs, improved residents' sense of security.

- Reduced Recidivism: Offenders who participated in the circles were less likely to re-offend, supported by community accountability and engagement.

Conclusion

Restorative justice circles offer a powerful alternative to traditional punitive measures within the criminal justice system. By focusing on repairing harm, fostering accountability, and supporting rehabilitation, these circles can reduce recidivism and promote healing for victims, offenders, and communities. Successful implementation involves building awareness and support, training facilitators, establishing clear procedures, creating a safe and inclusive environment, and integrating circles into justice processes. Through thoughtful planning and consistent application, restorative justice circles can transform the criminal justice system, promoting justice, empathy, and community resilience.

CHAPTER 13

CULTURAL AND GLOBAL PERSPECTIVES ON RESTORATIVE JUSTICE CIRCLES

Restorative justice circles are practiced worldwide, reflecting diverse cultural adaptations and demonstrating their universal applicability and adaptability. This chapter highlights global perspectives and practices, showcasing how different cultures integrate restorative justice principles into their traditions and justice systems. By examining these practices, we can gain a deeper understanding of the flexibility and effectiveness of restorative justice circles across various cultural contexts.

The Universality of Restorative Justice

Restorative justice principles resonate universally because they address fundamental human needs for healing, accountability, and community cohesion. While the specific practices may vary, the core values of empathy, respect, and mutual support are common across different cultures. This universality allows restorative justice circles to be adapted to diverse cultural contexts while maintaining their effectiveness.

Cultural Adaptations of Restorative Justice Circles

1. Indigenous Practices in North America:

- Peacemaking Circles: Many Indigenous communities in North America have long traditions of using circles for conflict resolution and community decision-making. These peacemaking circles emphasize the interconnectedness of individuals and the community.

- Holistic Approach: Indigenous restorative practices often incorporate spiritual and cultural elements, such as prayers, rituals, and the use of symbolic objects like a talking stick, to create a sacred space for dialogue.

2. Marae Justice in New Zealand:

- Māori Traditions: In New Zealand, restorative justice circles are deeply rooted in Māori traditions. The Marae, a communal and sacred meeting place, serves as the setting for restorative justice processes.

- Whānau Involvement: The involvement of whānau (extended family) and community members is crucial, reflecting the Māori value of collective responsibility and support.

3. Ubuntu Philosophy in South Africa:

- Ubuntu: The African philosophy of Ubuntu, which emphasizes interconnectedness, humanity, and compassion, underpins restorative justice practices in South Africa.

- Community Justice: Restorative justice circles in South Africa often involve the broader community in addressing harm and finding collective solutions, reflecting the communal nature of Ubuntu.

4. Restorative Justice in Japan:

- Chōtei: In Japan, the concept of chōtei (mediation) aligns with restorative justice principles. This approach focuses on reconciliation and mutual agreement, often facilitated by community leaders or respected mediators.

- Harmony and Apology: Japanese restorative practices emphasize harmony and the importance of sincere apologies in restoring relationships and social balance.

5. Restorative Practices in Europe:

- Family Group Conferencing: Originating in New Zealand, family group conferencing has been widely adopted in Europe, particularly in the United Kingdom and the

Netherlands. This model involves the family and social network of the offender in the restorative process.

- Victim-Offender Mediation: Many European countries, such as Germany and Norway, have integrated victim-offender mediation into their justice systems, providing a structured space for dialogue and resolution.

Case Studies of Global Restorative Justice Practices

Case Study 1: Peacemaking Circles in Canada

Background: An Indigenous community in Canada experienced ongoing conflicts related to land disputes. Traditional justice systems were not effective in resolving the deeply rooted issues.

Implementation:

- Peacemaking Circles: The community implemented peacemaking circles, facilitated by Elders and respected community members. The circles included all affected parties and were conducted in a sacred space with cultural rituals.

- Circle Process: Participants shared their perspectives and the impact of the disputes on their lives. The Elders guided the dialogue, emphasizing respect, empathy, and collective responsibility.

- Agreements: The circles resulted in agreements for shared land use, community projects to strengthen bonds, and ongoing circles for conflict prevention.

Outcome:

- Restored Relationships: The peacemaking circles restored relationships and trust within the community.

- Sustainable Solutions: The agreements provided sustainable solutions that respected cultural traditions and addressed the community's needs.

Case Study 2: Marae-Based Restorative Justice in New Zealand

Background: In a Māori community in New Zealand, a young person committed a crime that caused significant harm. The traditional justice system's punitive approach was not aligned with the community's values.

Implementation:

- Marae Justice: The community chose to address the harm through a marae-based restorative justice circle. The circle involved the offender, the victim, their whānau, and community leaders.

- Circle Process: The circle was conducted on the marae, with cultural rituals and prayers. Participants shared their experiences, and the whānau provided support and accountability for the offender.

- Agreements: The circle resulted in agreements for restitution, cultural education for the offender, and community service.

Outcome:

- Whānau Support: The involvement of whānau and the community provided strong support for the offender's rehabilitation.

- Restored Balance: The restorative process restored balance and harmony within the community, aligning with Māori values.

Case Study 3: Ubuntu-Inspired Restorative Justice in South Africa

Background: A South African community faced a series of thefts that eroded trust and safety. The formal justice system's approach did not address the community's broader needs for healing.

Implementation:

- Ubuntu Circles: The community implemented restorative justice circles inspired by Ubuntu philosophy. The circles included offenders, victims, and community members.

- Circle Process: The circles were facilitated by community leaders, emphasizing interconnectedness and compassion. Participants shared their experiences and discussed the broader impact of the thefts.

- Agreements: The circles resulted in agreements for restitution, community projects, and ongoing circles to foster community cohesion.

Outcome:

- Community Healing: The Ubuntu circles facilitated collective healing and strengthened community bonds.

- Reduced Recidivism: Offenders were supported in their rehabilitation, reducing the likelihood of reoffending.

The Adaptability of Restorative Justice Circles

Restorative justice circles are adaptable to various cultural contexts because they can be tailored to reflect the values, traditions, and practices of different communities. Key elements that support this adaptability include:

1. Cultural Sensitivity: Understanding and respecting the cultural context of participants is crucial for the success of restorative justice circles.

2. Community Involvement: Engaging the community in the process ensures that the solutions are culturally relevant and supported.

3. Flexibility in Process: The circle process can be adjusted to incorporate cultural rituals, symbols, and practices that resonate with the participants.

4. Focus on Core Values: Despite cultural differences, the core values of empathy, respect, and mutual support remain central to restorative justice circles.

Conclusion

Restorative justice circles demonstrate their universal applicability and adaptability through diverse cultural practices around the world. By integrating cultural traditions and values, these circles effectively address harm, promote healing, and strengthen community bonds. Whether through peacemaking circles in Indigenous communities, marae-based justice in New Zealand, Ubuntu-inspired practices in South Africa, or mediation in Japan, restorative justice circles provide a powerful framework for justice that resonates across cultures. By embracing cultural diversity and focusing on core restorative values, restorative justice circles can create meaningful and lasting positive change globally.

CHAPTER 14

BUILDING AND SUSTAINING RESTORATIVE COMMUNITIES

Creating and maintaining a restorative community requires ongoing effort, commitment, and collaboration. This chapter provides guidance on sustaining restorative practices, fostering community involvement, and ensuring the longevity of restorative justice circles. By building a strong foundation and continually nurturing restorative principles, communities can create an environment where healing, accountability, and mutual support thrive.

Foundations of a Restorative Community

1. Shared Vision and Values:

- Collective Vision: Establish a shared vision of what a restorative community looks like, involving all stakeholders in the process.

- Core Values: Identify and promote core values such as empathy, respect, accountability, and inclusivity that guide all restorative practices.

2. Community Engagement:

- Inclusive Participation: Ensure that all community members have opportunities to participate in restorative practices and decision-making processes.

- Stakeholder Involvement: Engage diverse stakeholders, including schools, local organizations, law enforcement, and businesses, to build a network of support.

3. Education and Awareness:

- Restorative Justice Education: Provide ongoing education and training on restorative justice principles and practices to community members.

- Awareness Campaigns: Use awareness campaigns to inform the community about the benefits and impact of restorative justice circles.

Sustaining Restorative Practices

1. Consistent Implementation:

- Regular Circles: Schedule regular restorative justice circles to address conflicts, build relationships, and maintain a restorative culture.

- Integration into Systems: Integrate restorative practices into existing systems, such as schools, workplaces, and the criminal justice system.

2. Training and Development:

- Facilitator Training: Continuously train new facilitators and provide ongoing professional development for existing ones.

- Skill Development: Offer skill development workshops on active listening, conflict resolution, and cultural competence for community members.

3. Resource Allocation:

- Funding and Support: Secure funding and resources to support restorative justice initiatives, including facilitator training, circle logistics, and educational materials.

- Infrastructure: Develop infrastructure to support restorative practices, such as designated spaces for circles and access to necessary materials.

Fostering Community Involvement

1. Building Relationships:

- Community Building Circles: Conduct regular community building circles to strengthen relationships, foster trust, and promote a sense of belonging.

- Collaborative Projects: Initiate collaborative projects that bring community members together to work towards common goals, enhancing mutual support.

2. Empowerment and Leadership:

- Empowering Individuals: Empower individuals to take active roles in restorative practices by providing leadership opportunities and recognizing their contributions.

- Leadership Development: Develop leadership programs that train community members to become restorative justice advocates and facilitators.

3. Communication and Transparency:

- Open Communication: Foster open and transparent communication within the community about restorative justice initiatives, progress, and challenges.

- Feedback Mechanisms: Establish feedback mechanisms that allow community members to share their experiences, provide input, and suggest improvements.

Ensuring Longevity of Restorative Justice Circles

1. Evaluation and Adaptation:

- Regular Evaluation: Conduct regular evaluations of restorative justice circles to assess their effectiveness, identify areas for improvement, and celebrate successes.

- Adaptation and Innovation: Adapt practices based on feedback and evolving community needs, and be open to innovative approaches that enhance restorative outcomes.

2. Institutional Support:

- Policy Integration: Advocate for the integration of restorative justice principles into local policies and regulations to ensure long-term support and sustainability.

- Institutional Partnerships: Build partnerships with institutions, such as schools, justice systems, and social services, to embed restorative practices within their frameworks.

3. Community Ownership:

- Shared Responsibility: Foster a sense of shared responsibility for maintaining and promoting restorative practices within the community.

- Sustainability Planning: Develop sustainability plans that outline long-term goals, strategies, and resources needed to sustain restorative justice circles.

Case Studies of Sustaining Restorative Communities

Case Study 1: Restorative School District

Background: A school district implemented restorative justice circles to address conflicts and improve school culture. The initial success led to efforts to sustain and expand these practices.

Implementation:

- Consistent Implementation: The district scheduled regular circles for conflict resolution, community building, and peer support.

- Training and Development: Teachers, staff, and students received ongoing training in restorative practices, with new facilitators trained each year.

- Community Engagement: The district engaged parents, local organizations, and law enforcement in restorative initiatives, creating a broad support network.

Outcome:

- Improved School Culture: The consistent implementation of circles improved relationships, reduced conflicts, and fostered a positive school culture.

- Sustainable Practices: The integration of restorative practices into the district's policies and the continuous training of facilitators ensured the longevity of the initiatives.

Case Study 2: Restorative Community Organization

Background: A community organization aimed to build a restorative community through regular circles and collaborative projects. The organization focused on engaging diverse stakeholders and fostering community ownership.

Implementation:

- Community Building Circles: The organization conducted regular community building circles to strengthen relationships and promote mutual support.

- Collaborative Projects: Initiated collaborative projects, such as neighborhood cleanups and cultural celebrations, to bring community members together.

- Leadership Development: Developed leadership programs to train community members as restorative justice advocates and facilitators.

Outcome:

- Enhanced Community Bonds: The community building circles and collaborative projects enhanced relationships and fostered a strong sense of community.

- Sustained Engagement: The leadership programs empowered community members to take ownership of restorative practices, ensuring sustained engagement and support.

Case Study 3: Institutionalized Restorative Justice

Background: A city government sought to institutionalize restorative justice practices within its local justice system to reduce recidivism and support rehabilitation.

Implementation:

- Policy Integration: The city integrated restorative justice principles into its local policies and regulations, ensuring long-term support for restorative practices.

- Institutional Partnerships: Built partnerships with schools, social services, and law enforcement to embed restorative practices within their frameworks.

- Resource Allocation: Secured funding and resources to support restorative initiatives, including facilitator training and circle logistics.

Outcome:

- Reduced Recidivism: The integration of restorative justice practices into the local justice system led to reduced recidivism rates and improved rehabilitation outcomes.

- Institutional Support: The partnerships and policy integration provided strong institutional support, ensuring the sustainability of restorative justice practices.

Conclusion

Building and sustaining restorative communities requires ongoing effort, commitment, and collaboration. By establishing a shared vision, engaging the community, providing education and training, and integrating restorative practices into existing systems, communities can create an environment where healing, accountability, and mutual support thrive. Through consistent implementation, fostering community involvement, and ensuring institutional support, restorative justice circles can be sustained over the long term, promoting a culture of empathy, respect, and collective well-being.

CHAPTER 15

FUTURE DIRECTIONS FOR RESTORATIVE JUSTICE CIRCLES

The field of restorative justice is continually evolving, adapting to new challenges and opportunities in our rapidly changing world. This chapter explores emerging trends, potential advancements, and future directions for restorative justice circles, envisioning their expanding role in promoting healing and justice. By embracing innovation and addressing contemporary issues, restorative justice circles can continue to be a powerful tool for fostering empathy, accountability, and community cohesion.

Emerging Trends in Restorative Justice Circles

1. Technology Integration:

- Virtual Circles: The use of digital platforms to conduct virtual restorative justice circles has increased, especially in response to the COVID-19 pandemic. This trend allows for greater accessibility and participation from diverse locations.

- Online Training: The availability of online training for facilitators and participants has expanded, making restorative justice education more accessible and scalable.

2. Expanding Applications:

- Environmental Justice: Restorative justice circles are being applied to address environmental harm and conflicts related to natural resources, promoting sustainable and community-centered solutions.

- Workplace Wellness: Beyond conflict resolution, restorative justice circles are being used to enhance workplace wellness, address systemic issues, and build a positive organizational culture.

3. Intersectionality and Inclusivity:

- Cultural Sensitivity: There is a growing emphasis on integrating cultural sensitivity and intersectionality into restorative justice practices, ensuring that circles are inclusive and respectful of diverse identities and experiences.

- Gender and Racial Justice: Restorative justice circles are increasingly being used to address gender and racial injustices, creating spaces for marginalized voices and promoting equity.

Potential Advancements in Restorative Justice Circles

1. Research and Evaluation:

- Data-Driven Practices: Advancements in research and evaluation methods can enhance the effectiveness of restorative justice circles by providing data-driven insights and best practices.

- Impact Assessment: Developing comprehensive frameworks for assessing the long-term impact of restorative justice circles on individuals and communities will help in refining and improving practices.

2. Policy Integration:

- Legislative Support: Advocating for policies that support the integration of restorative justice principles into legal and institutional frameworks can provide sustainable funding and structural support.

- Restorative Schools and Communities: Implementing restorative justice practices at systemic levels within schools and communities can institutionalize these practices and ensure their longevity.

3. Innovative Practices:

- Trauma-Informed Approaches: Integrating trauma-informed approaches into restorative justice circles can enhance their effectiveness, particularly for participants with a history of trauma.

- Hybrid Models: Combining restorative justice circles with other restorative practices, such as restorative conferencing and mediation, can provide more comprehensive solutions to complex conflicts.

Future Directions for Restorative Justice Circles

1. Global Expansion and Adaptation:

- Cross-Cultural Learning: Promoting cross-cultural learning and exchange of restorative justice practices can enrich the field and adapt successful models to different cultural contexts.

- International Collaborations: Strengthening international collaborations can support the global expansion of restorative justice circles and create a unified movement for restorative justice.

2. Education and Youth Engagement:

- Restorative Education Programs: Developing restorative education programs in schools and universities can nurture a new generation of restorative justice practitioners and advocates.

- Youth-Led Initiatives: Encouraging youth-led restorative justice initiatives can empower young people to take active roles in promoting justice and healing within their communities.

3. Community Empowerment and Sustainability:

- Community-Led Circles: Supporting community-led restorative justice circles can enhance community ownership and sustainability of restorative practices.

- Capacity Building: Investing in capacity building for communities, including training and resources, can ensure the effective and sustained implementation of restorative justice circles.

4. Integration with Social Movements:

- Restorative Justice and Social Movements: Aligning restorative justice circles with broader social movements, such as movements for racial justice, gender equality, and environmental sustainability, can amplify their impact and reach.

- Collaborative Advocacy: Engaging in collaborative advocacy with social movements can promote systemic change and address root causes of injustice.

Case Studies of Innovative Restorative Justice Practices

Case Study 1: Virtual Restorative Justice Circles

Background: A community faced challenges in conducting in-person restorative justice circles due to the

COVID-19 pandemic. The need for accessible and safe conflict resolution practices led to the adoption of virtual circles.

Implementation:

- Digital Platforms: The community utilized digital platforms to conduct virtual restorative justice circles, ensuring that participants could join from their homes.

- Online Training: Facilitators received online training on conducting virtual circles and using digital tools effectively.

Outcome:

- Increased Accessibility: Virtual circles increased accessibility for participants who could not attend in-person sessions due to distance or health concerns.

- Continued Engagement: The community maintained engagement in restorative practices despite the pandemic, promoting ongoing healing and resolution.

Case Study 2: Environmental Restorative Justice

Background: A rural community experienced conflict over natural resource management, leading to environmental degradation and strained relationships.

Implementation:

- Environmental Circles: The community implemented restorative justice circles focused on environmental justice, involving local stakeholders, environmental experts, and affected residents.

- Collaborative Solutions: Participants discussed the environmental harm, and its impact, and collaboratively developed sustainable solutions for resource management.

Outcome:

- Sustainable Practices: The circles resulted in sustainable resource management practices that balanced environmental preservation with community needs.

- Restored Relationships: Relationships among community members improved, fostering a collective commitment to environmental stewardship.

Case Study 3: Youth-Led Restorative Justice Initiatives

Background: A high school sought to empower students to take active roles in promoting justice and healing within their school community.

Implementation:

- Youth Circles: The school supported the formation of youth-led restorative justice circles, with students trained as facilitators and leaders.

- Peer Mediation: Students engaged in peer mediation through restorative circles to address conflicts and promote a positive school culture.

Outcome:

- Empowered Students: Students felt empowered and took ownership of the restorative justice process, leading to increased engagement and responsibility.

- Positive School Culture: The youth-led initiatives contributed to a positive and inclusive school culture, with reduced conflicts and improved relationships.

Conclusion

The future of restorative justice circles is bright, with emerging trends and potential advancements offering new opportunities for growth and impact. By embracing technology, expanding applications, and integrating innovative practices, restorative justice circles can adapt to contemporary challenges and continue to promote healing and justice. The global expansion of restorative justice, combined with community empowerment and alignment with social movements, can create a powerful force for positive change. Through education, youth engagement, and sustained community involvement, restorative justice circles will remain a vital tool for fostering empathy, accountability, and community cohesion in a changing world.

www.ingramcontent.com/pod-product-compliance
Lightning Source LLC
Chambersburg PA
CBHW061244120726
48001CB00001B/130